Tax Morale II

BUILDING TRUST BETWEEN TAX ADMINISTRATIONS AND LARGE BUSINESSES

OECD

BETTER POLICIES FOR BETTER LIVES

This work is published under the responsibility of the Secretary-General of the OECD. The opinions expressed and arguments employed herein do not necessarily reflect the official views of the Member countries of the OECD.

This document, as well as any data and map included herein, are without prejudice to the status of or sovereignty over any territory, to the delimitation of international frontiers and boundaries and to the name of any territory, city or area.

Please cite this publication as:
OECD (2022), *Tax Morale II: Building Trust between Tax Administrations and Large Businesses*, OECD Publishing, Paris, https://doi.org/10.1787/7587f25c-en.

ISBN 978-92-64-32068-0 (print)
ISBN 978-92-64-81553-7 (pdf)
ISBN 978-92-64-91103-1 (HTML)
ISBN 978-92-64-98656-5 (epub)

Foreword

A better understanding of what motivates individual and business taxpayers to participate in, and comply with, a tax system is valuable for all countries and stakeholders. Tax administrations can benefit from increased compliance and higher revenues, taxpayers are better served by tax systems that are responsive to their needs, while increased data and discussion can help researchers deepen their understanding and identify possible solutions to improving tax compliance. Other stakeholders may also benefit, including investors seeking to influence companies to engage in responsible business conduct when setting their tax policies, civil society groups advocating for improved tax policies and development partners looking to maximise the impact of development assistance.

The OECD's tax morale workstream aims to encourage research, dialogue and actions to deepen the understanding of tax morale as well as the policies that enhance it. Tax morale, most concisely defined as the intrinsic motivation to pay tax, is complex and dynamic, varying across countries and taxpayers, as well as over time. The OECD work on tax morale seeks to help countries navigate some of this complexity by providing new research, convening and participating in multi-stakeholder discussions, and collating and disseminating good practices. Previous work has examined the role of institutional and socio-economic factors in determining tax morale as outlined in *Tax Morale: What Drives People and Businesses to Pay Tax?*, and has created a typology of taxpayer education initiatives together with examples of best practices explained in *Building Tax Culture, Compliance and Citizenship: A Global Source Book on Taxpayer Education, Second Edition.*

This report complements and builds on previous work, providing a specific focus on tax morale and multinational enterprises (MNEs). While the tax affairs of MNEs have been the subject of increased attention in recent years, there has been relatively little focus on tax morale among MNEs. This has started to change with the growing importance for investors and MNEs of Environmental, Social and Governance (ESG) considerations, and the inclusion of taxation in ESG criteria and reporting for MNEs. This report seeks to further deepen the understanding of MNE tax morale and the policies that can influence it, and it intends to stimulate and encourage further research and discussion on this topic. On the basis of this work, the OECD will seek to actively contribute to the growing global dialogue on MNE tax morale.

While tax morale is a topic of global interest, it is especially important for developing countries, where tax revenues are lower as a proportion of GDP than in OECD economies and where tax morale is currently lower. The importance of tax revenues for development has been highlighted by both the Sustainable Development Goals (SDGs) and the Addis Ababa Action Agenda on financing for development. Tax revenues are the largest source of financing for development, providing the funds governments need to invest in relieving poverty, delivering public services and building the physical and social infrastructure for long-term development. Increasing tax revenues is therefore an essential objective for developing countries as they seek to raise the additional financing needed to realise the SDGs. At the same time, research suggests that tax morale is low in many developing countries (see *Tax Morale: What Drives People and Businesses to Pay Tax?*); identifying policies that can increase tax morale is therefore especially important for developing countries with low tax morale.

This report was written by René Orozco, Julia Soto Alvarez and Joseph Stead of the OECD Centre for Tax Policy and Administration, under the supervision of Ben Dickinson, Head of the Global Relations and Development Division of the Centre for Tax Policy and Administration. Valuable assistance was provided by Nawal Ali, Zipporah Gakuu, Karena Garnier, Hazel Healy, Alex Pick, Adriana Ruiz Esparza, Natalie Lagorce, Iratxe Sáenz de Villaverde and Carrie Tyler. The report was also informed by discussions at four regional roundtables, organised in partnership with the African Tax Administration Forum, the Asian Development Bank, the Intra-European Organisation of Tax Administrations, and the Inter-American Center of Tax Administrations. The authors would like to thank all the participants of the roundtables for their contribution, and to thank the four partner organisations for their co-operation in these events, and for valuable feedback provided on early drafts of this report.

This report was produced with the financial assistance from the governments of Ireland, Japan, Luxembourg, the Netherlands, Norway, Sweden, Switzerland, and the United Kingdom. The contents of this report do not necessarily reflect the official views of any of these governments.

Table of contents

FIGURES

TABLES

BOXES

Follow OECD Publications on:

https://twitter.com/OECD

https://www.facebook.com/theOECD

https://www.linkedin.com/company/organisation-eco-cooperation-development-organisation-cooperation-developpement-eco/

https://www.youtube.com/user/OECDiLibrary

https://www.oecd.org/newsletters/

Acronyms and abbreviations

ACCT	Collaboration Agreements for Tax Compliance
ACT	Collaboration Agreements
ADB	Asian Development Bank
APA	Advanced Pricing Agreements
ATAF	African Tax Administration Forum
BEPS	Base Erosion and Profit Shifting
BIAC	Business Industry Advisory Committee
Big Four	Deloitte, EY, KPMG and PricewaterhouseCoopers
CbC	Country-by-Country
CIAT	Inter-American Center of Tax Administrations
DGI	Direction générale des Impôts (Côte d'Ivoire)
DIAN	Dirección de Impuestos y Aduanas Nacionales (Colombia)
ESG	Environmental, Social and Governance
GTCC	Global Tax Code of Conduct
HMRC	Her Majesty's Revenue and Customs (United Kingdom)
HQ	Headquarter
ICAP	International Compliance Assurance Programme
IMF	International Monetary Fund
IOTA	Intra-European Organisation of Tax Administrations
ISORA	International Survey on Revenue Administration

KRA	Kenya Revenue Authority
LAC	Latin America and the Caribbean
MNE	Multinational Enterprises
NCP	National Contact Points
OECD	Organisation for Economic Co-operation and Development
PwC	PricewaterhouseCoopers
SDG	Sustainable Development Goals
SEZs	Special Economic Zones
SGATAR	Study Group on Asian Tax Administration and Research
SII	Servicio de Impuestos Internos (Chile)
SME	Small and Medium Size Enterprises
TCF	Tax Control Frameworks
TIWB	Tax Inspectors Without Borders
TPP	Tax Policy Panels
VAT	Value Added Tax

Executive summary

The taxation of large businesses, and especially Multinational Enterprises (MNEs), has been a high priority globally for a number of years. Updating the international tax rules to ensure that governments are better able to tax MNEs in the era of globalisation and digitalisation has been on the international political agenda since the global financial crisis. This prioritisation has led to a number of important reforms, including the update in 2011 of the OECD Guidelines for Multinational Enterprises (OECD, 2011[1]), which call on MNEs to comply with both the letter and spirit of the laws and regulations of the countries in which they operate, the OECD/ G20 Base Erosion and Profit Shifting (BEPS) Actions agreed in 2015, and the landmark agreement reached in October 2021 on the two-pillar solution to addressing the tax challenges of the digitalising economy, joined by 137 members of the OECD/G20 Inclusive Framework on BEPS (hereafter Inclusive Framework).

The focus on international tax policy has been accompanied by increased attention from the public, media and investors on the tax practices and tax morale of MNEs. In many countries, MNEs have been subject to increased public and media scrutiny concerning their tax practices. Furthermore, a growing number of investors are concerned about aggressive tax planning by the companies they invest in and are screening MNEs on their approach to fulfilling their tax obligations as part of their Environmental, Social and Governance (ESG) considerations. In many cases, especially as part of ESG, such scrutiny seeks to hold MNEs accountable not only to the letter of the law, but also to the spirit of the law, thereby encouraging higher tax morale (the intrinsic willingness to pay tax) among MNEs.

While there is a growing interest in the tax morale of MNEs, there is relatively limited research on the topic. While the body of research on tax morale has increased in recent years, much of this has focused on individuals, rather than on trying to understand what factors may influence the tax morale of businesses, especially MNEs, how tax morale may vary across countries and regions, and how it can be enhanced.

To help address this gap, this report builds on previous research of MNE perceptions of government performance to deliver tax certainty, with an examination of the perceptions of tax administrators concerning MNEs' performance against voluntary commitments on best practices. The 2019 report *Tax Morale: What Drives People and Businesses to Pay Tax?* (OECD, 2019[2]) used data on MNEs perceptions on tax certainty to identify some potential determinants of MNE tax morale. To complement the perceptions from MNEs, some 1 240 tax officials from 138 jurisdictions participated in an online survey to provide their perceptions of MNE adherence to the *Business at OECD (BIAC) Statement of Tax Best Practices for Engaging with Tax Authorities in Developing Countries* (Business at OECD, 2013[3]). The results of both perception surveys were subsequently discussed at a series of regional roundtables that brought together tax administrations and MNEs.

By combining these data sets, this report identifies not only how MNEs' adherence to best practices across different regions is perceived but also the factors that may influence tax morale, especially the key issue of trust between MNEs and tax administrations. Trust is increasingly recognised as a key driver of tax morale and is more responsive to policy interventions than many other factors (Dom et al., 2022[4]), making it a useful lens through which to analyse tax morale. By bringing together the perceptions of business and tax administrations, this report seeks to focus on mutual trust and how to build it. It further seeks to focus on those areas where businesses and tax administrations have identified common challenges, indicating a shared interest in adopting new approaches.

The data underlying this report shows that business behaviour is perceived more positively in OECD countries and in Asia than in Africa and in Latin America and the Caribbean (LAC). Behaviour is perceived to be better on more routine compliance and formal co-operation than on more subjective issues, such as trust in information and transparency. There is wide variation in tax officials' perceptions of MNE behaviour, both regionally and according to topic. While in all regions there are some officials who perceive consistently good adherence to best practices across most large businesses/MNEs, this is much more common in the OECD and to a lesser extent in Asian countries than in African or LAC countries. In all regions, officials perceive that most large businesses/MNEs perform routine compliance well (e.g. paying on time) and are at least formally co-operative. Perceptions are significantly less positive in all regions with regard to openness and transparency displayed by business and trust in the information they provide, especially so across Africa and the LAC region.

Government officials' perceptions of the behaviour of the 'Big Four' professional services networks (Deloitte, EY, KPMG, and PricewaterhouseCoopers) were similar to their perceptions concerning MNEs but with less variation between regions. While there was less variation between the regions when questions were asked on perceptions of Big Four behaviour, similar patterns to the perceptions of MNEs were observed. For example, the Big Four were generally seen to be formally co-operative but were much less likely to be seen to follow the spirit/intention of the laws, or to only promote tax planning aligned with substance.

These results, together with the roundtable discussions between tax administrations and MNEs, highlight a lack of mutual trust and sub-optimal communication between tax administrations and businesses. The survey results were discussed at a series of regional roundtables which brought together tax administration officials and businesses to provide further context. These roundtables confirmed the survey's finding that trust and communication were key challenges, and highlighted the impact that poor relationships between tax administrations and businesses can have, creating costs and inefficiencies on both sides. It is in the interests of tax administrations and businesses to invest in improving this dynamic. Tax administrations will be better able to prioritise their limited resources, enabling enforcement actions to be more accurately targeted at those most non-compliant, while compliant businesses will benefit from greater certainty and reduced compliance burdens.

There is no single solution to building trust and improving communication to increase tax morale. The required combination of actions will depend on the country context, but in all cases, it will require commitments from both tax administrations and businesses to succeed. While co-operative compliance (OECD, 2016[5]) is seen by many, especially MNEs, as the preferred relationship between tax administrations and MNEs, it is not something that can be established quickly. It requires high levels of pre-existing trust and commitment to openness and transparency. Co-operative compliance may be a logical goal for the relationship with MNEs in many countries, but it may not be the starting point for all. In many countries the best starting point may be to identify practical steps to improve communication, which can be built upon progressively.

This report outlines a range of existing good practices as well as new opportunities, highlighted by both MNEs and tax administrations in the regional roundtables. The actions suggested in chapter three of this report do not purport to represent an exhaustive list of actions but rather a reflection of the discussions, especially those that identified convergence between MNEs and tax administrations on actions that had already proved useful or had the potential to address some of the challenges identified. Nor do they seek to prescribe what should happen in each context, since this will be determined by local circumstances (and resources). Instead, they seek to provide options for both administrations and businesses to consider. These actions range from the relatively simple (e.g. increasing use of local languages when filing and communicating with the tax administration), to the more complex (e.g. establishing tax ombudsmen). The discussions also identified scope to improve/expand existing initiatives (e.g. improve the statement of tax best practices) or establish new initiatives (e.g. developing a process for a voluntary multilateral dialogue). The list of actions is not exhaustive, although it is hoped that the classification of types of actions (compliance and audit strategies, expectations/accountability of behaviour, transparency and communication, and capacity building programmes) will help all stakeholders in identifying the best approaches for each specific context. While the focus of the discussions during the roundtables was on policies and practices that would improve the situation with respect to MNEs, many of the good practices identified may help build trust and tax morale with all taxpayers.

While the issues highlighted are relevant globally, this report focuses primarily on developing countries, which are more reliant on tax revenues from large businesses, suffer from greater tax avoidance and face larger capacity challenges. Developing countries are not only more reliant on corporate income tax than OECD countries but are also especially reliant on large taxpayers. Data from the International Survey on Revenue Administration (ISORA) shows that the Large Taxpayers Units in Africa were responsible for administering 64% of total revenues in 2019 (over twice the level as the OECD at 31%). Developing countries are also estimated to suffer relatively more from international tax avoidance, with an estimated cost of 1.3% of GDP, compared with 1% of GDP in OECD countries (Crivelli and De Mooij, 2015[6]). The impact of these revenue losses is even more significant given the lower tax-to-GDP ratios in developing countries.

The OECD will continue to identify ways to support both tax administrations and MNEs in building trust, improving communication and increasing tax morale. While the onus is primarily on MNEs, as well as tax administrations to take actions to build trust, the OECD will seek to identify how it can be supportive. This is likely to include further research, integrating some of the findings from this report into OECD capacity building, developing further guidance and case studies on issues highlighted by the report, and identifying opportunities where the involvement of the OECD as a third party can help build trust and strengthen relationships between MNEs and tax authorities.

More broadly, the OECD will also continue to encourage research, dialogue and innovation on tax morale, especially in developing countries, to help deliver the tax systems necessary to achieve the Sustainable Development Goals (SDGs). This report is part of the OECD's broader work on tax morale, which undertakes new research and encourages global discussions on various aspects of tax morale, especially in developing countries. Covering both businesses and individuals, this workstream recognises the importance of considering tax morale as part of the debate on tax policy and administration, as building tax systems with strong societal support and promoting voluntary compliance will be vital for delivering development that is sustainable in the long term.

References

Business at OECD (2013), *BIAC Statement of Tax Best Practices for Engaging with Tax Authorities in Developing Countries*, https://biac.org/wp-content/uploads/2020/11/Statement-of-Tax-Best-Practices-for-Engaging-with-Tax-Authorities-in-Developing-Countries-Original-release-Sep-2013-1.pdf. [3]

Crivelli, E. and R. De Mooij (2015), *Base Erosion, Profit Shifting and Developing Countries: IMF Working Paper WP/15/118*, https://www.imf.org/external/pubs/ft/wp/2015/wp15118.pdf. [6]

Dom, R. et al. (2022), *Innovations in Tax Compliance: Building Trust, Navigating Politics, and Tailoring Reform*, World Bank Group, http://hdl.handle.net/10986/36946. [4]

OECD (2021), *Building Tax Culture, Compliance and Citizenship: A Global Source Book on Taxpayer Education, Second Edition*, OECD Publishing, Paris, https://doi.org/10.1787/18585eb1-en. [7]

OECD (2019), *Tax Morale: What Drives People and Businesses to Pay Tax?*, OECD Publishing, Paris, https://doi.org/10.1787/f3d8ea10-en. [2]

OECD (2016), *Co-operative Tax Compliance: Building Better Tax Control Frameworks*, OECD Publishing, Paris, https://doi.org/10.1787/9789264253384-en. [5]

OECD (2011), *OECD Guidelines for Multinational Enterprises, 2011 Edition*, OECD Publishing, https://doi.org/10.1787/9789264115415-en. [1]

1 Introduction

This introductory chapter indicates the importance of MNE tax morale, especially in developing countries, and highlights the value of a focus on trust when considering tax morale. It also summarises the data on which the rest of the report is based.

While there has been growing research on tax morale, there has been relatively little focus on tax morale issues in MNEs and their role in building a taxpaying culture. Tax morale, or the intrinsic willingness to pay tax, is a vital part of tax systems, as all tax systems rely on voluntary compliance from most taxpayers. Previous research (OECD, 2019[1]) highlighted that while there is growing data and research available on tax morale in individuals, there is very little research that looks at businesses and almost nothing focussed on MNEs.

Improving tax morale, and by extension improving compliance, of MNEs operating in developing countries offers significant potential for increasing revenues. Developing countries are, on average, more reliant on corporate income tax than developed countries. In 2019, corporate income tax accounted for 20.1% of total tax revenues in the Asia-Pacific region, 19.2% in Africa, 15.5% in the LAC region and 10% in the OECD (OECD, 2021[2]), with MNEs being the largest source of corporate income tax. MNEs also pay significant amounts of indirect taxes and they often act as withholding agents for taxes of their employees. In many cases, MNEs are therefore responsible for a large proportion of the tax base; for example, MNEs recently accounted for 70% of Rwanda's tax base, while a single MNE was responsible for 20% of Burundi's total tax revenue (ATAF, 2016[3]). Improving the compliance of MNEs therefore offers the potential for governments to collect higher revenues with less enforcement effort, thereby enabling limited enforcement resources to be more efficiently deployed against those with low tax morale. As such, improving tax morale can make an important contribution to enhancing financing for sustainable development and achievement of the SDGs.

Trust is a useful entry point for examining tax morale, including for MNEs. This report brings together data sets to enable a more detailed examination of trust and the factors affecting trust between MNEs and tax administrations. There is a growing body of research highlighting trust as one of the key factors behind tax morale (see (Dom et al., 2022[4])). As trust is conditional and thus can be responsive to policy changes, it is a good place to start when examining the phenomenon and identifying actions to enhance it. To do so, this report brings together data from perception surveys of both tax administrations and MNEs; these perceptions provide valuable insights into current levels of trust and show possible ways in which trust, and by extension tax morale, can be increased.

This report uses a unique new data set of perceptions among tax administration officials concerning how large businesses/MNEs are adhering to one of the most widely endorsed voluntary principles. This data set has been obtained through a global survey that collected responses from 1 240 tax officials from 138 jurisdictions. This survey asked for perceptions of large business/MNE behaviour against the *Business at OECD (BIAC) Statement of Best Practices for Engaging with Tax Authorities in Developing Countries* (Business at OECD, 2013[5]), which was endorsed by BIAC in 2013. BIAC is a global network that collectively represents over seven million companies of all sizes. These principles therefore represent a broad consensus from business on what constitutes best practice. Thus while they may not include all aspects that could be examined, they provide a useful starting point for examining perceptions of business behaviour against practices that businesses have themselves endorsed. The survey also asked for perceptions of behaviour of the Big Four accountancy firms against a composite of voluntary tax principles published by some of the Big Four.

The tax administration officials' perceptions are complemented by additional data from a previous survey on MNE perceptions on tax certainty and joint business/tax administration roundtables. Previous work by the OECD identified MNE perceptions on tax certainty as a useful indicator of tax morale and found that effective and efficient tax administration is likely to enhance compliance and morale among MNEs (OECD, 2019[1]). Both these surveys were then discussed at a series of roundtables held between December 2020 and May 2021. The virtual roundtables were organised on a regional basis (Africa, Asia, Europe and LAC) in collaboration with regional organisations: the African Tax Administration Forum (ATAF), the Asian Development Bank (ABD), the Intra-European Organisation of Tax Administrations (IOTA), and the Inter-American Center of Tax Administrations (CIAT). The roundtables were provided with a background document providing the main results from the surveys on both tax administration and MNE perceptions, and they discussed the factors that might explain the survey results as well as good practices and further actions that could help build tax morale. These discussions are reflected in the analysis of the results in chapter two, and form the basis for the range of possible actions in chapter three. As the discussions were held under the Chatham House Rule, interventions made during the roundtables are not attributed.

This report examines trust between MNEs and tax administrations, a key driver of tax morale, and highlights a range of actions that can help build tax morale. The perceptions of MNE behaviour give an overall indication of MNE tax morale. In addition, by comparing the two sets of survey data, and discussing the results at the roundtables, it has been possible to place the results in a broader context and identify not only the level of trust but also factors that may be important for building (or inhibiting) trusted relationships, such as transparency and communication. It has also been possible to identify areas where tax administrations and MNEs identify common challenges (albeit from different perspectives), suggesting that there may be mutual interest in adopting new approaches.

Not all taxpayers will be responsive to the measures set out in this report; enforcement has a crucial role to play. This report focuses on taxpayers who are responsive to efforts to improve tax morale, and especially measures to build trust. For those that are not responsive, other actions will be needed to encourage compliance. Thus while this report focuses on tax morale, and especially how trust (and the facilitation of trust) can help build the willingness for voluntary compliance, enforcement will always remain a vital component of compliance (see (Dom et al., 2022[4]) for further detail on the interaction between trust, facilitation and enforcement). Similarly, while this report focuses primarily on actions by tax administrations and businesses, there are a wider range of stakeholders (including investors and civil society) who have a role to play in influencing the tax morale of businesses and who have different tools at their disposal to those identified in this report.

While improving tax morale and strengthening the relationship between taxpayers and tax administrations should reduce disputes, it will not eradicate them. Disputes over tax can emerge for a range of reasons, and while many of these can be addressed (as this report will highlight), reducing the number of disputes, it is not possible to eliminate disputes entirely. Especially in complex areas of taxation (such as international tax) there can be legitimate differences in interpretation, which require a dispute process to resolve. Where disputes emerge, it is desirable that they are resolved effectively, with all parties accepting the validity of differing positions and the outcome, without adverse effects on their trust in the other parties or their willingness to maintain a positive relationship in the future.

This report seeks to provide an entry point for further dialogue and discussion on how to measure, track and build trust and tax morale in large businesses/MNEs, especially in developing countries. While some of the good practices and suggestions for further actions identified in the report are not necessarily new, the report may encourage increased engagement from all parties in seeking solutions to improve tax morale by providing new empirical evidence and emphasising the importance of tax morale.

References

ATAF (2016), *African Tax Outlook*, https://events.ataftax.org/index.php?page=documents&func=view&document_id=15#.   [3]

Business at OECD (2013), *BIAC Statement of Tax Best Practices for Engaging with Tax Authorities in Developing Countries*, https://biac.org/wp-content/uploads/2020/11/Statement-of-Tax-Best-Practices-for-Engaging-with-Tax-Authorities-in-Developing-Countries-Original-release-Sep-2013-1.pdf.   [5]

Dom, R. et al. (2022), *Innovations in Tax Compliance: Building Trust, Navigating Politics, and Tailoring Reform*, World Bank Group, http://hdl.handle.net/10986/36946. [4]

OECD (2021), *Revenue Statistics in Asia and the Pacific 2021: Emerging Challenges for the Asia-Pacific Region in the COVID-19 Era*, OECD Publishing, Paris, https://doi.org/10.1787/ed374457-en. [2]

OECD (2019), *Tax Morale: What Drives People and Businesses to Pay Tax?*, OECD Publishing, Paris, https://doi.org/10.1787/f3d8ea10-en. [1]

2 Results and analysis

This chapter presents new data on tax administrations perceptions of MNE and Big Four behaviour. In analysing this data it is combined with previous data on MNE perceptions of tax systems, and the results of roundtable discussions between tax administration officials and business representatives in different regions.

2.1. Overview

In all regions, routine compliance by large business/MNE/Big Four is generally perceived to be good. However, in more complex and subjective interactions, including trust in information, transparency and openness, behaviour is generally perceived more negatively, with significant variation between regions. Especially in LAC and Africa, tax officials perceive significant challenges with the relationships with MNEs, suggesting tax morale can be improved, although it is notable that officials perceive a high willingness to co-operate when disputes have arisen in all regions. The results from the survey of tax administration perceptions of large business/MNE/Big Four behaviour also show wide variation in perceptions of how power and incentives are used, including concerning minorities perceiving illegal behaviour by business. Figure 2.1 provides an aggregated summary of the results for perceptions of large business/MNE behaviour. In this figure, the results have been normalised from one to five, where five is the best possible outcome. The figure compares simple regional averages for selected variables and groups them in five sub-indexes, presenting their corresponding average. The sub-indexes cover routine compliance; co-operation and trust; openness and transparency; disputes, conflict and resolution; and use of power and incentives. This chapter comprises a section on each sub-index. It also includes sections on two additional issues covered in the survey, staff recruitment, and comparison with local businesses. Detailed results can be found in Annex A and the methodology in Annex C.

Figure 2.1. Overview of authorities' perception of the tax behaviour of large businesses

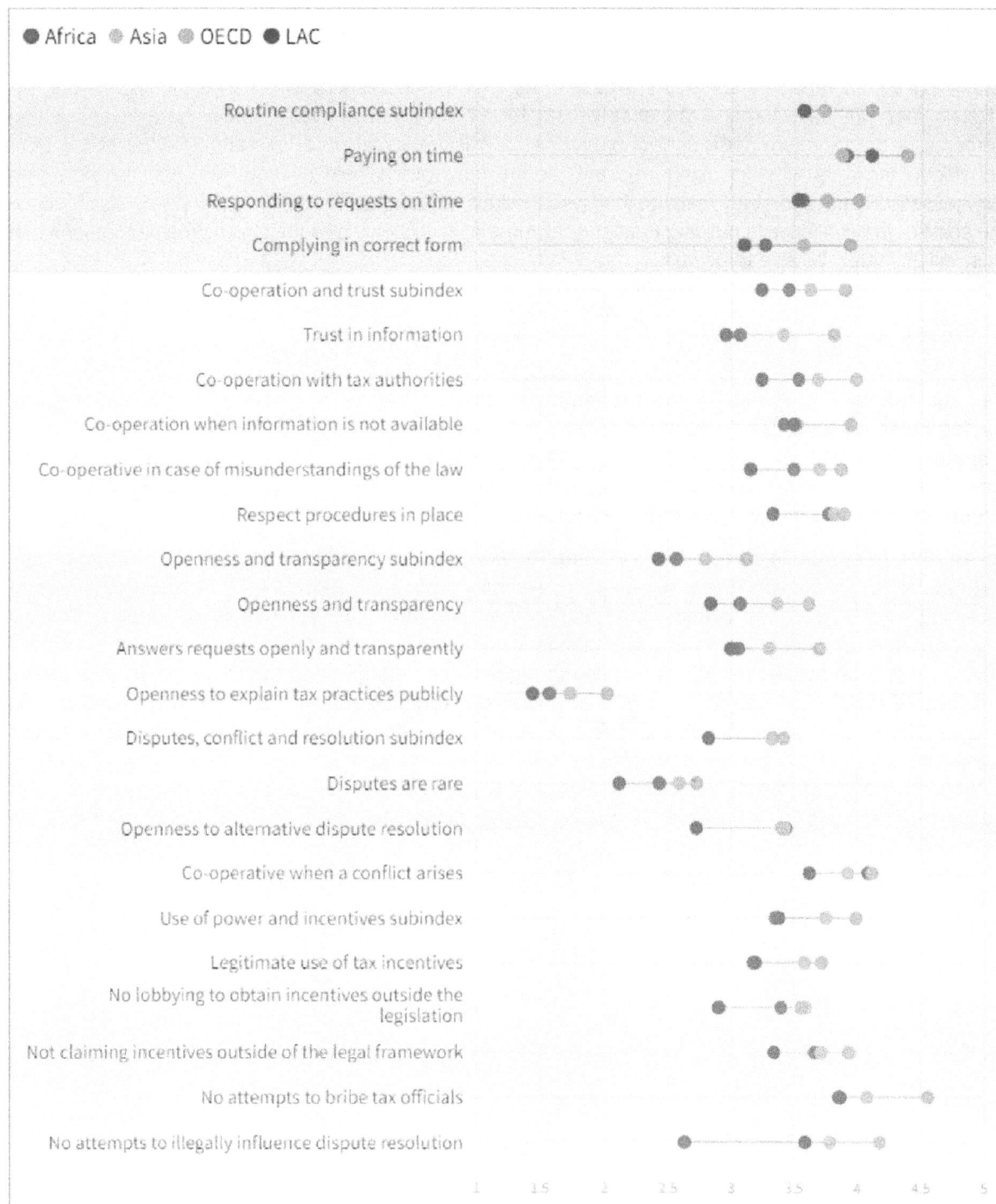

Note: Simple regional average. Values range from 1 to 5, with 5 being the best score possible. Countries are weighted so that no country represents more than 10% of a regional sample.
Source: OECD (2020), Survey on MNEs and Big Four Firms tax behaviour.

While perception surveys are subject to limitations, they are crucial to understanding the relationships between tax administrations and taxpayers. There are well known challenges in using perception surveys, especially in tax, where respondents are often found to behave differently to how they say they will. Some of these challenges are less relevant in this analysis, given the focus is on the perceived behaviour of others, rather than the behaviour of the respondents themselves. There are additional risks however, not least that perceptions of the behaviour of others are skewed by the most memorable experiences of the respondents (either positive or negative) with a small number of actors, rather than a balance of all relevant experience. In the case of reported perceptions by tax officials of the Big Four, tax officials may not have direct experience of the Big Four's client services. While there is a risk that perceptions are therefore not a perfect proxy for the existing levels of tax morale of MNEs or Big Four behaviour, the data remains highly relevant, as the perceptions held by both tax administrators and businesses will affect how they manage their relationships with each other. These perceptions also indicate the scale of the challenge in building trust and tax morale, as it is only through shifting the perceptions that trust will ultimately be able to be built.

2.2. Routine compliance

Tax administrations across all regions generally have a positive perception of MNEs as regards paying taxes on time. Timely payment of taxes is fundamental to voluntary compliance. In this respect, there was a fairly uniform perception across all regions that large businesses/MNEs pay their tax liabilities within the established due date, with at least 77% of tax officials across all regions agreeing that most or almost all MNEs pay on time (Figure 2.2, Panel A).

As routine interactions become more complex, perceived compliance begins to diverge across regions. MNEs performance is less well perceived with respect to responding to requests on time and providing information in the correct form, both of which are also routine functions of compliance. In all regions, perceived performance was lower than for paying on time: in the OECD, the proportion of officials saying most large businesses/MNEs respond to requests on time dropped to 75%, while in Asia, Africa and the LAC region, between 65% and 50% of officials answered that most or all MNEs responded on time (Figure 2.2, Panel B). Similarly, perceptions of whether information is provided in the correct form exhibit significant heterogeneity across regions: in the LAC region, less than half (44%) of tax authorities believe that most or all large businesses/MNEs provide the information requested in the correct form. This percentage rises to 54 % in Africa, 61% in Asia and 75% in the OECD.

Figure 2.2. Do large businesses/MNEs pay/answer on time?

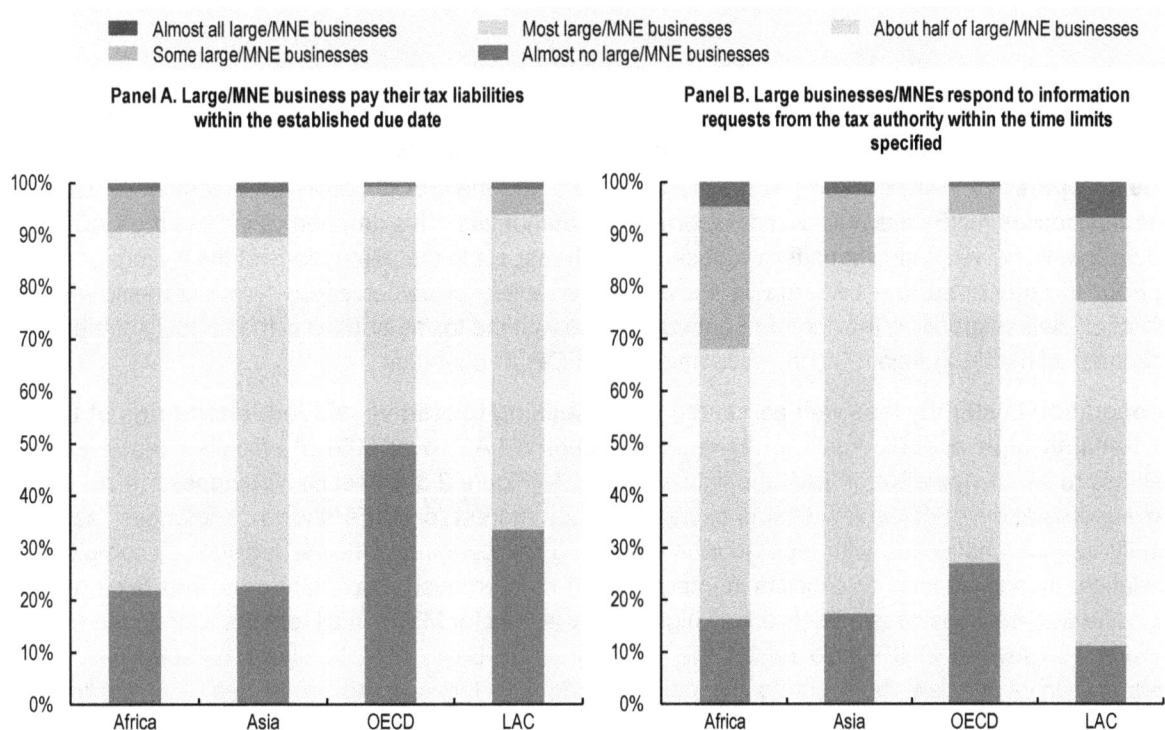

Legend:
- Almost all large/MNE businesses
- Most large/MNE businesses
- About half of large/MNE businesses
- Some large/MNE businesses
- Almost no large/MNE businesses

Panel A. Large/MNE business pay their tax liabilities within the established due date

Panel B. Large businesses/MNEs respond to information requests from the tax authority within the time limits specified

Note: Simple regional average. Countries are weighted so that no country represents more than 10% of their regional sample.
Source: OECD (2020), Survey on MNEs and Big Four Firms tax behaviour.

While there was agreement from MNEs and tax administrations that no reasonable requests for information can be refused, both the roundtables and the survey of MNE perceptions identified challenges to responding to such requests. These included obstacles within businesses as well as in the ways in which information is requested.

The (un)predictability of requirements for taxpayers may affect their ability to respond on time. During the roundtables, several MNEs noted the challenges they face in responding on time when they receive requests without warning and/or with short deadlines, especially if they arrive at busy times for tax compliance, such as at the end of the tax year. Business indicated that their response to requests is often slowed down by factors such as the level of detail of the requests, the use of a language different to that used for internal communication, the format in which data is requested (when it is different from the one in which the company keeps its records) and barriers for accessing information held by other entities within the group. While most of these factors can be addressed by businesses improving their own processes and providing sufficient resourcing to enhance compliance, there are some areas where tax administrations may be able to encourage more effective responses by adjusting how and when they request information.

Businesses also raised questions about the purpose and efficiency of some requests, indicating that a prior understanding of what the administration wishes to analyse would improve their ability to comply and would reduce compliance burdens. Administrations agreed that higher compliance was observed when taxpayers were able to understand 'why' they have been asked for certain information. The opinions expressed during the roundtable discussions are supported by data from the survey on MNEs, where unpredictable or inconsistent treatment from the authorities was among the biggest concerns of MNEs (1st out of 21 factors in Asia, 2nd in LAC, 3rd in Africa and 6th in the OECD). The level of bureaucracy (including documentation requirements) is also a major concern (1st in LAC, and OECD, 2nd in Asia and 4th in Africa), in line with the roundtable discussions.

2.3. Co-operation and trust

Tax officials outside the LAC region generally perceived MNEs/large businesses and the Big Four to be co-operative. Over 60% of officials in Africa, Asia and the OECD perceived that most or almost all large businesses/MNEs are willing to co-operate with authorities. This dropped to 49% in the LAC region (Figure 2.3, Panel A). A similar pattern is observed with respect to the perceptions of the willingness of the Big Four to co-operate: the LAC region showed lower levels of perceived co-operativeness, with only 27% of officials responding that the Big Four co-operate with the tax authorities in the majority of the cases, in contrast with 45% in Asia, 50% in Africa and 58% in OECD countries.

Co-operation is slightly less well perceived when seeking to resolve misunderstandings of the law but remains high overall. Again, in all regions except in LAC, over 60% of officials considered most business to be co-operative; in LAC the figure was 48% (Figure 2.3, Panel B). Willingness to co-operate in misunderstandings of the law seems to be of mutual interest to MNEs and tax authorities, as MNEs identify various challenges with legislation in achieving tax certainty. Unclear legislation, complexity in legislation, inconsistencies or conflicts in interpretation of international tax standards, and tax legislation not in line with new business models are all high priority issues for MNEs in all regions. During the regional roundtables, several MNEs also raised the importance of being able to share perspectives on the interpretation of the law, both during the policymaking and the auditing processes. The challenge is especially marked in LAC, as while MNEs operating in LAC rate issues of misunderstanding of the law a higher concern than any other region, tax administrations in the LAC region perceive a lower willingness to co-operate to address such misunderstandings.

Figure 2.3. Large businesses/MNEs willingness to cooperate

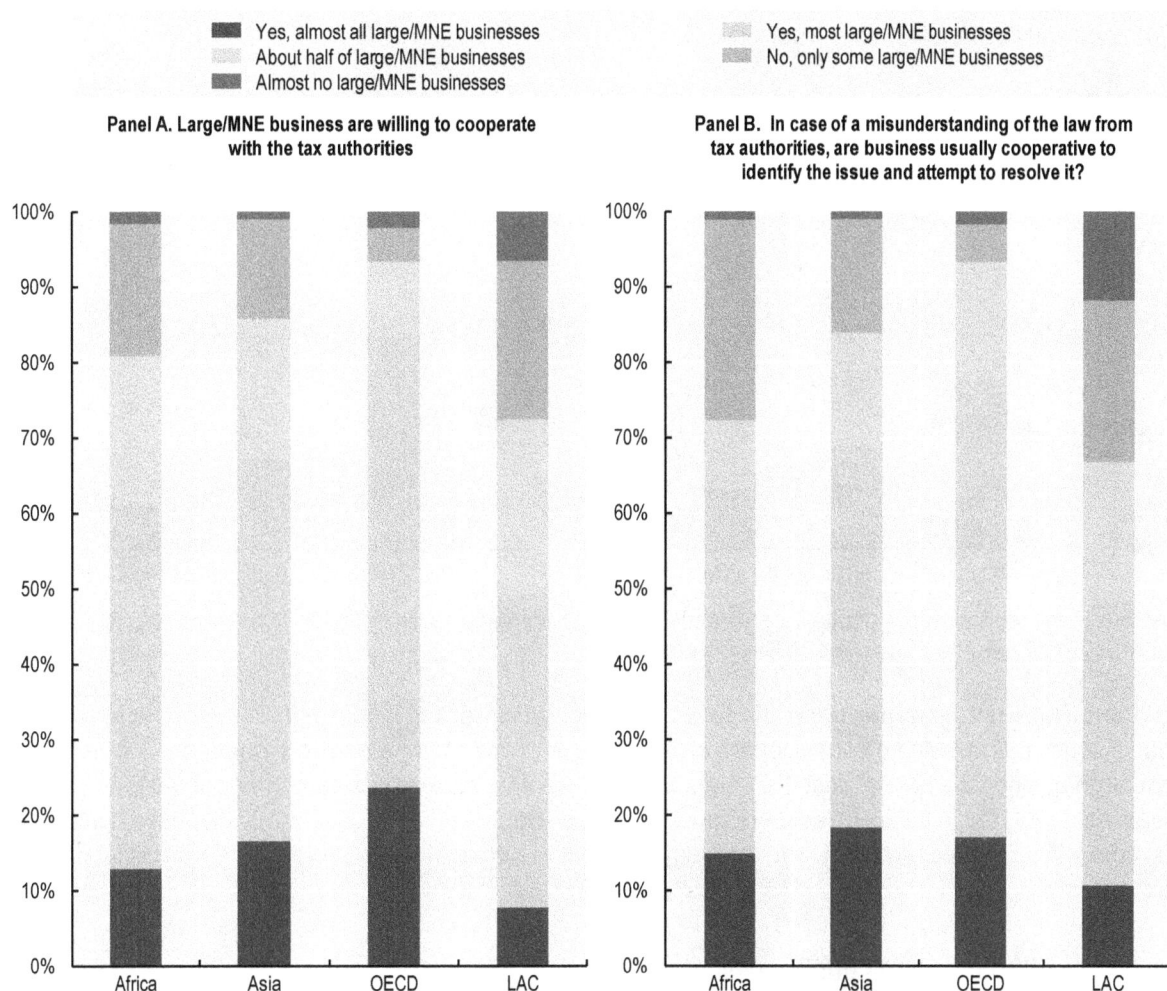

Legend:
- Yes, almost all large/MNE businesses
- Yes, most large/MNE businesses
- About half of large/MNE businesses
- No, only some large/MNE businesses
- Almost no large/MNE businesses

Panel A. Large/MNE business are willing to cooperate with the tax authorities

Panel B. In case of a misunderstanding of the law from tax authorities, are business usually cooperative to identify the issue and attempt to resolve it?

Note: Simple regional average. Countries are weighted so that no country represents more than 10% of their regional sample.
Source: OECD (2020). Survey on MNEs and Big Four Firms tax behaviour.

Perceptions of willingness to co-operate are lower when information is not available. When asked how frequently companies provide justification for not providing information and collaborate with the authorities, only around 50% of tax officials in Africa, Asia and LAC respond that in most cases they receive a justification and observe a collaborative attitude (Figure 2.4). This is significantly lower than in the OECD countries (78%), and suggests that access to information may be a particular challenge in Asia, Africa and LAC, something that the roundtables appeared to confirm. Several administrations pointed that the challenges increase when information is held by another entity within the same MNE group, a point also highlighted by several business participants in the roundtables.

Figure 2.4. MNE/large business reaction to request of information by the tax authorities

When information requested by the tax authorities was not available from the taxpayer, they provided a justified explanation and collaborated with the authorities

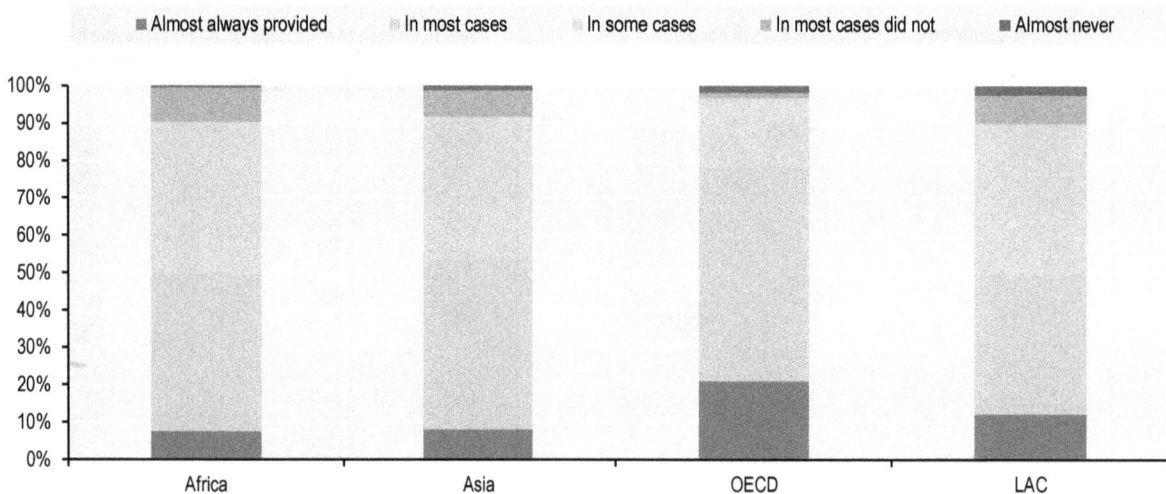

Note: Note: Simple regional average. Countries are weighted so that no country represents more than 10% of their regional sample.
Source: OECD (2020), Survey on MNEs and Big Four Firms tax behaviour.

Co-operation may increase once disputes emerge. When asked about perceptions on co-operation when discussing/resolving disputes, only a small share of tax officials perceived a non-cooperative attitude from large businesses/MNEs. Just 5% of officials in Africa saw businesses as non-cooperative in some/all cases, rising to 17% in the LAC region (Figure 2.5). This suggests that once a formal dispute exists, MNEs are more willing to co-operate; in turn, this suggests that the potential exists to promote this attitude before disputes arise.

Figure 2.5. Attitude of large businesses/MNE in resolving disputes

In your experience, when discussing/seeking to resolve disputed issues with large businesses/MNEs, the attitude of large businesses/MNEs has been

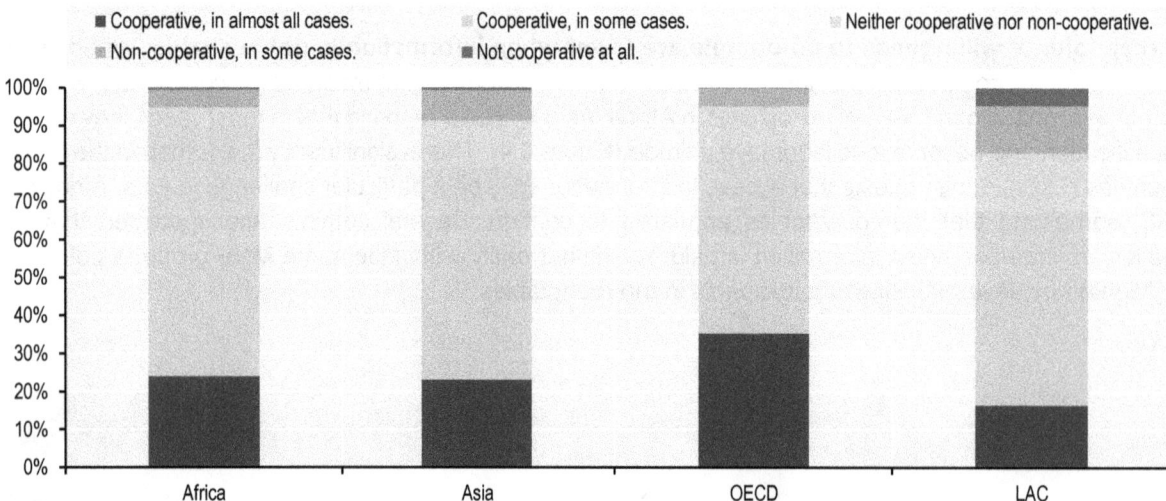

Note: Simple regional average. Countries are weighted so that no country represents more than 10% of their regional sample.
Source: OECD (2020), Survey on MNEs and Big Four Firms tax behaviour.

Co-operation does not appear to be synonymous with trust. While tax officials may perceive large businesses/MNEs as being co-operative, that does not necessarily mean that tax officials see co-operation as being based on trust, especially regarding trust in the information provided. When officials were asked whether the tax information provided by large MNEs could be trusted, the responses were far less positive than perceptions of co-operation, especially outside the OECD. While 74% of officials from OECD countries say the information from most/all large businesses/MNEs can be trusted, this falls to 53% in Asia, 43% in Africa and 37% in the LAC region. Similarly, while most tax officials see large businesses/MNEs as being co-operative during disputes, a much lower proportion perceive business to be acting in good faith during dispute negotiations (see Disputes, conflict and resolution). This lack of trust between tax administrations and businesses was raised repeatedly in the roundtables, which identified finding approaches to (re)build trust to be a high priority for both tax administrations and business.

Figure 2.6. Trust in the information provided by large businesses/MNEs

The tax information provided by large businesses/MNEs to the tax authorities can be trusted

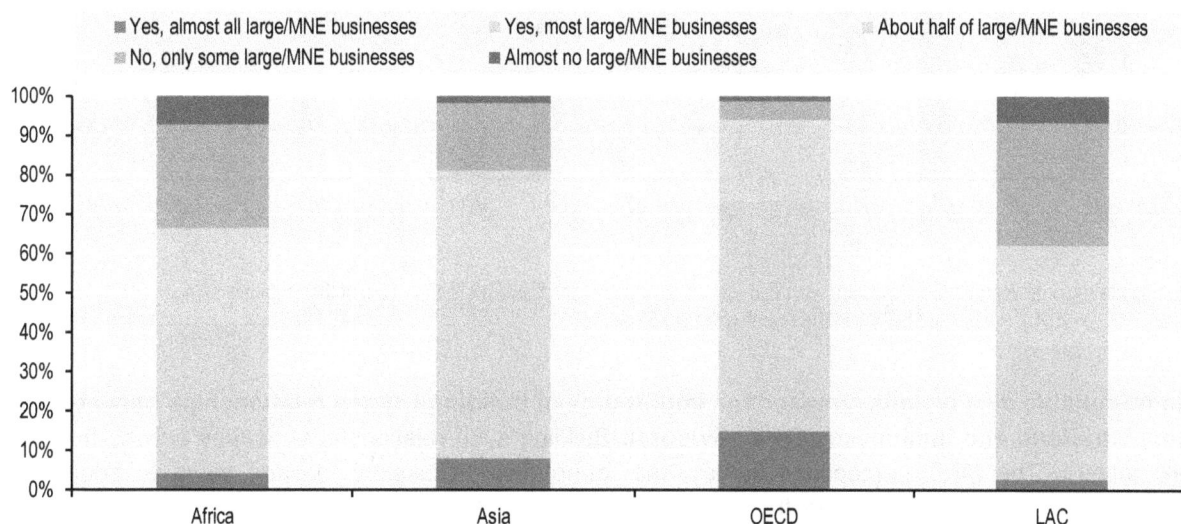

Note: Simple regional average. Countries are weighted so that no country represents more than 10% of their regional sample.
Source: OECD (2020), Survey on MNEs and Big Four Firms tax behaviour.

Perceived co-operation by the Big Four is not correlated with perceptions of following the spirit/intention of the law, or willingness to promote artificial tax planning structures. While around 50% of officials (except in the LAC region, where the proportion was 27%) said that the Big Four were co-operative with the authorities in the majority of cases (Figure 2.7, Panel A), this falls to around 25% (19% in LAC) when asked if the Big Four follow the spirit/intention of the tax laws Figure 2.7, Panel B). This may be a reflection that in many countries the tax laws are unclear, and discerning the spirit/intention of the tax laws can be challenging. A similar pattern, however, was seen in response to a question about whether the Big Four only promote tax planning aligned with substance (i.e. do not promote artificial tax-planning structures). Here the pattern was similar to responses on the spirit of the law, with around 20% of officials in Africa, Asia and the LAC region saying that the Big Four promote tax planning aligned with substance in the majority of cases (29% in the OECD) (Figure 2.7, Panel C). Again, there may be differences of opinion regarding substance requirements, but these results suggest that the challenges of building trust are also present in the relationship between tax authorities and the Big Four, at least in a common interpretation of the law.

Figure 2.7. Co-operation, following the spirit of the law and tax planning by the Big Four

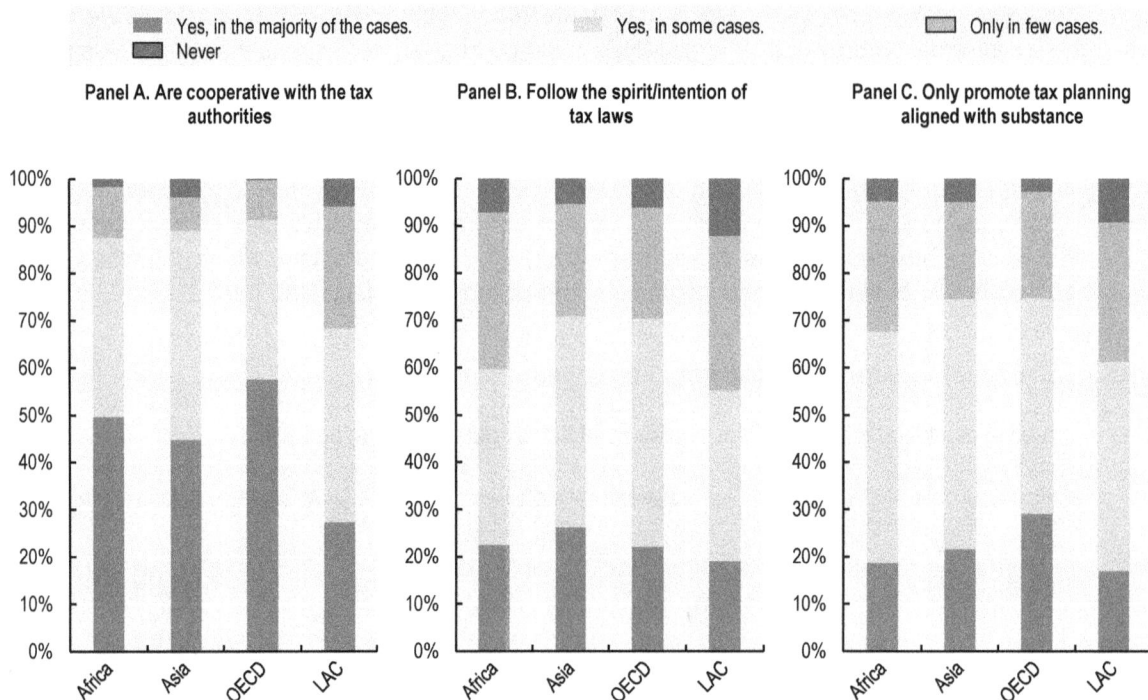

Note: Simple regional average. Countries are weighted so that no country represents more than 10% of their regional sample.
Source: OECD (2020), Survey on MNEs and Big Four Firms tax behaviour.

The roundtable discussions stressed the importance of building trusted relationships between tax administrations and businesses (and advisors). Building such relationships requires actions from all stakeholders. The MNE perceptions survey and roundtable discussions provide valuable additional information on the range of issues that need to be addressed to build trust. The results from the tax administration survey suggest that some businesses (and advisors) may need to review their approach to co-operation with tax administrations, especially those outside OECD countries, not only to focus on the formalities of co-operation but also to improve the quality of co-operation. This is unlikely to be sufficient however, given trust requires actions from all partners; as such the discussions in the roundtables and data from MNEs perceptions can provide valuable additional information on what might be hindering trust and help identify areas to focus on to build mutual trust.

MNEs do not perceive significant problems with their relationship with tax authorities in general. A 'general poor relationship with the tax authority' was one of the lowest ranked sources of tax uncertainty for MNEs operating in all regions, ranking 20th of 21 issues in Africa and the LAC region, 19th in Asia and 17th in the OECD. This suggests that, just as most tax officials consider most large businesses/MNEs to be co-operative (at least to some degree), most MNEs do not have a negative view of their overall relationship with tax authorities. This indicates there while there are a range of specific issues to address, there is a reasonably solid basis on which to build trust.

Unpredictable treatment by tax authorities may limit scope for co-operation and hinder trust. Unpredictable or inconsistent treatment by the tax authority was identified as the highest rated source of tax uncertainty in Asia, 2nd in LAC, 3rd in Africa and 6th in the OECD. It was also raised in the roundtables as an issue hindering trust and co-operation, with MNEs highlighting how it is difficult for them to be fully responsive and co-operative in an unpredictable environment.

Unclear legislation and/or considerable bureaucracy may also affect co-operation and trust. Where the requirements for compliance are unclear and/or there is excessive bureaucracy, it may be challenging for companies to fully co-operate. Unclear legislation was the highest rated source of tax uncertainty in Africa (2nd in the OECD, 8th in Asia and LAC), while the level of bureaucracy was the most important issue in LAC and OECD, 2nd in Asia and 4th in Africa.

MNEs also identify tax authorities' lack of understanding of value chains and concerns over international taxation as challenges to building effective relationships. In all roundtables, MNEs and tax administrations highlighted challenges around tax authorities' understanding of value chains, which can create confusion and miscommunication, leading to a perception of unwillingness to co-operate and/or lack of trust. Businesses noted this can be exacerbated by concerns over the implementation of international taxation (consistently in the top 10 sources of tax uncertainty for MNEs), where some MNEs noted that their willingness to co-operate can be reduced if they expect that their co-operation will result in treatment that deviates from international standards.

The organisational structure of tax administrations and MNEs affect taxpayers' willingness to co-operate. Some businesses noted that they felt reluctant to voluntarily share information in negotiations or consultations if they felt there was a risk that those sharing information voluntarily may end up at a greater risk of audit or other enforcement action than similar businesses that were less transparent. Several administrations declared that having different teams or agencies across which to separate the negotiation, auditing, and dispute resolution functions was effective in building trust and providing a sense of impartiality. The internal structure of MNEs might also have an effect: administrations reported better co-operation with large taxpayers that had specific internal governance structures for engaging with tax administrations.

Guidelines may be a useful tool to build trust. Where they exist, most tax officials think that large businesses/MNEs follow them. Guidelines can help clarify requirements and frame the relationship between taxpayers and tax administrations in a transparent and open manner. The surveys provide a range of evidence to support the use of guidelines. In Africa, Asia and the OECD, around 75% of tax officials see most large businesses/MNEs as following the existing guidelines/guidance/procedures for managing the relationship between tax authorities and taxpayers. This proportion drops to 58% in LAC.

There is also a correlation between respondents identifying the existence of specific procedures/guidelines to deal with MNEs and perceiving higher levels of trust in MNEs. Respondents who said that guidelines/procedures existed in their jurisdiction were more likely to perceive that all/most MNEs/large businesses were open and transparent, suggesting that there could be a link between guidelines and improved relationships between taxpayers and tax administrations. More than half (57%) of respondents that said that detailed procedures existed in their jurisdiction also perceived that all/most MNEs/large businesses are open and transparent.

More work may be needed however to ensure use and awareness of guidelines. The data also suggests that, where guidelines/procedures exist, there is a need to ensure their use. This is especially the case in the LAC region, where 29% of tax officials stated that they are almost never used (compared to around 10% in other regions). Efforts are also needed to raise awareness about them, for example, there was significant variance in responses from officials from the same administration on whether such guidelines exist, suggesting awareness within tax administrations is sometimes limited.

MNEs also prioritise guidance. MNEs operating in Africa rated detailed guidance on tax regulations as the most important tool to improve tax certainty, and it was ranked 3rd in Asia, 4th in the OECD and 6th in the LAC region. While this is not exactly the same kind of guidance tax administrators were surveyed on, it indicates that MNEs place a high value on good guidelines, which was further affirmed by MNEs participating in the roundtables. Some MNE participants also highlighted the value of taxpayers' charters and/or ombudsman functions to provide clarity and accountability on the relationship with tax administrators.

2.4. Openness and transparency

Perceptions on openness and transparency by large businesses/MNEs to tax authorities vary between regions. While 64% of officials in the OECD perceive most/all large businesses/MNEs to be open and transparent, providing all relevant information, that figure drops to 54% in Asia, 44% in Africa and only 32% in the LAC region (Figure 2.8). A similar pattern can be seen when looking at perceptions of transparency in response to requests: while 64% of officials in the OECD perceive most/all large businesses/MNEs answer requests in an open, transparent and straightforward manner, this drops to 48% in Asia, 43% in Africa and 38% in the LAC region (Figure 2.8).

Figure 2.8. Are large businesses/MNEs perceived to be open and transparent?

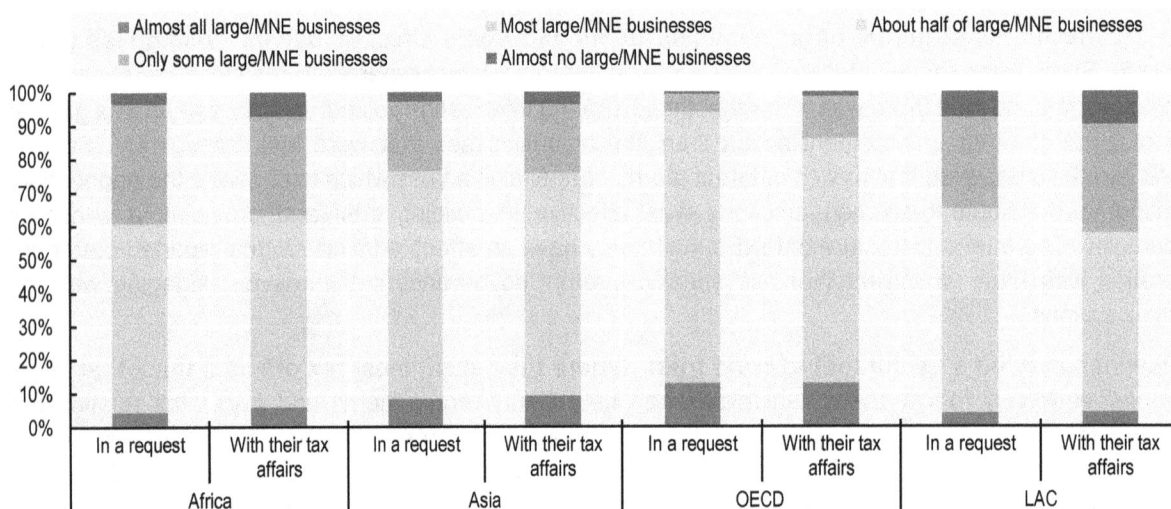

Note: 'In a request' refers to the question "Against the request of tax authorities, large/MNE business answer the tax authorities in an open transparent and straightforward manner". Similarly with tax affairs refers to the question "When thinking about the large/MNE business in your country, are the following statements accurate? Large/MNE business are open and transparent with the revenue authorities with their tax affairs, and relevant information". Countries are weighted so that no country represents more than 10% of their regional sample.
Source: OECD (2020), Survey on MNEs and Big Four Firms tax behaviour.

Perceptions of the willingness of large businesses/MNEs to publicly explain their tax practices also vary significantly between regions. Most tax officials are unaware of instances where which large businesses/MNEs have been asked to publicly explain their tax practices. 68% of officials in the LAC region were unaware of such requests in their country, while 61% in Africa, 56% in Asia and 38% in the OECD were similarly unaware. Given there has been much public debate and scrutiny of MNE tax practices in the media, parliaments and civil society in OECD countries, this discrepancy is perhaps unsurprising. Where officials are aware of demands for public discussion of corporate tax practices perceptions differ significantly between regions (Figure 2.9). Around two thirds of officials in OECD and Asia expressing a view see companies as willing to explain in most cases. This drops to just under half in Africa and a third in LAC. It is notable that in the regions where there is greater awareness of requests for public discussion of corporate tax practices, there is also a greater perception of willingness from companies to explain their practices. This may suggest that public pressure on companies to discuss their tax practices positively affects their willingness to engage in public discussion.

Figure 2.9. Willingness of large businesses/MNEs to explain their tax practices publicly

In my experience, in my country, when asked to explain their tax practices publicly (i.e. to the media, civil society, parliament) the approach of large businesses/MNEs has been

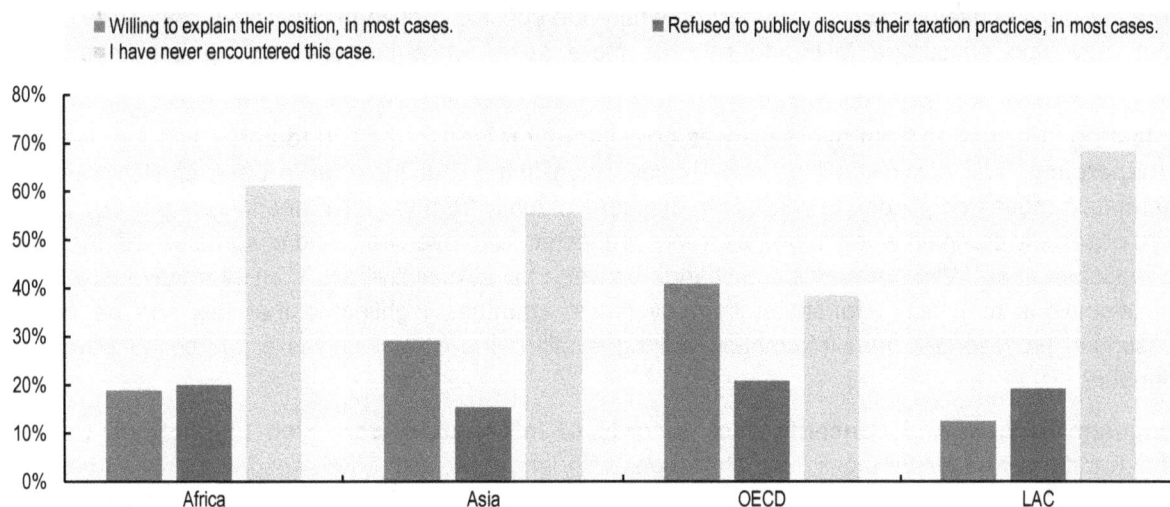

Note: Simple regional average. Countries are weighted so that no country represents more than 10% of a regional sample.
Source: OECD (2020), Survey on MNEs and Big Four Firms tax behaviour.

There is much less variation in perceptions of transparency among the Big Four. In contrast to the significant variation on perceptions of transparency of large businesses/MNEs, there is a much more uniform pattern when looking at perceptions of the Big Four. Some 31% of officials in OECD countries consider that the Big Four are transparent and provide all the relevant information when requested in the majority of cases. This proportion is 27% in Asia, 26% in Africa and 18% in the LAC region (Figure 2.10).

Figure 2.10. Perception of transparency of the Big Four firms with tax authorities

Big Four firms in my jurisdiction are transparent with the tax authorities, providing all relevant information when requested

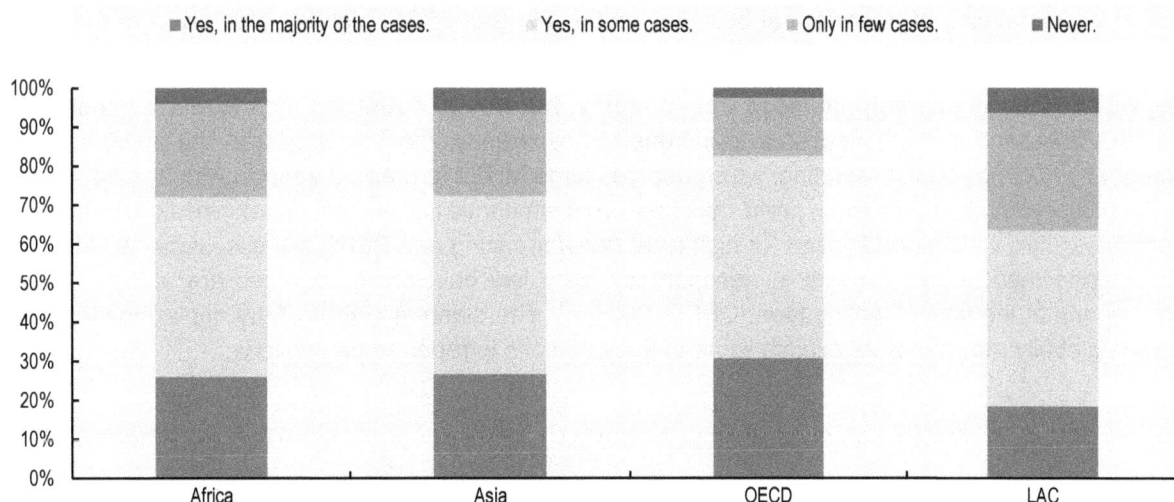

Note: Simple regional average. Countries are weighted so that no country represents more than 10% of their regional sample.
Source: OECD (2020), Survey on MNEs and Big Four Firms tax behaviour.

While legal requirements can enforce a degree of transparency, promoting openness is a two-way process. The roundtables and MNE perceptions survey identified that there may be mutual interest in reforms to improve openness and transparency. While taxpayers should comply with legal requirements for disclosure, such requirements alone are unlikely to develop a willingness to disclose, especially beyond the legal requirements. The discussions in the roundtables, and the data from the MNE perceptions survey therefore provide useful additional context on where the specific challenges may lie in transparency, and what may help encourage MNEs to become more open, while not undermining the need of tax administrations for information.

Obtaining information from overseas was consistently raised in the roundtables as a key issue on transparency. Tax administrations in all regions highlighted that there were often challenges where information requested needed to come from overseas (usually from the MNE headquarters (HQ)). Delays were especially common when information was requested from overseas, and in some cases, there was no response at all. While information exchange between tax administrations is an alternative way for tax administrations to obtain information from overseas, countries highlighted that this can be a time-consuming process, and that information-sharing is still being established in a number of developing countries.

Language barriers and concerns over security of information were also highlighted. Both tax administrations and MNEs highlighted challenges with language, with MNEs (especially when providing information from overseas) preferring to provide information in English, while many non-Anglophone tax administrations noted the challenges when information is provided in English, even when this is not permitted by the regulations. Another concern that hinders transparency is security of information; businesses highlighted that there needs to be confidence in data security safeguards if sensitive information is to be more willingly shared.

High levels of documentation requirements are one of the main concerns of MNEs. While documentation can be an important tool to enhance transparency, considerable bureaucracy, including documentation requirements, was the top concern for MNEs operating in OECD and the LAC region, second in Asia and fourth in Africa. In the roundtable discussions, MNEs highlighted that they were especially concerned about requirements for information where either the purpose is unclear – making it difficult to know what information to provide – or where the type or format of information requested does not appear to match the purpose – requiring more information to be prepared than necessary and/or increasing the likelihood that further requests will be necessary. In some cases, MNEs highlighted that this problem was linked to a lack of understanding of how the business operated, including how the value chain is structured. This concern was also noted to some degree in the tax certainty survey, with MNEs citing lack of understanding of international business as the 7th (out of 21) highest rated concern for MNEs operating in Africa, 11th in Asia, 14th in the LAC region and 10th in the OECD.

The BEPS Actions can help increase transparency, but not all countries are currently benefitting. The BEPS Actions include measures to increase transparency, most notably with the introduction of Country-by- Country (CbC) reporting, which requires large MNEs to prepare a report with aggregate data on the global allocation of income, profit, taxes paid and economic activity among tax jurisdictions in which it operates. This CbC report is used for high level transfer pricing and BEPS risk assessments. Although CbC reports mark a step forward in transparency, very few developing countries are able to receive CbC reports at the time of writing (see (OECD, 2021[1])). The different stages of the application of BEPS Actions globally may therefore explain some of the variations in reported perceptions.

2.5. Disputes, conflict and resolution

Across regions, tax disputes are fairly common. While disputes are an inevitable part of the tax system, frequent disputes may be both a sign of, and cause of, weaker trust between MNEs and tax authorities, and thus lower voluntary compliance. Disputes were fairly common in all regions, with fewer than 9% of tax officials saying that disputes never or rarely occurred. In the LAC region, 67% of tax authorities stated that disputes occurred almost always or very often, which was considerably higher than in Africa (48%), Asia (43%), and the OECD (32%). Especially notable is that 27% of the tax officials in the LAC region believe that tax disputes arise almost always, significantly higher than any other region (Figure 2.11, Panel A). While disputes are to be expected in any tax system, and perhaps especially when dealing with the complex international tax aspects of MNEs, very high frequency of disputes is a cause for concern, not least for the pressures this places on taxpayers and tax administrations. MNEs openness towards dispute resolution procedures could be improved across regions, with LAC showing again the lowest levels (Figure 2.11, Panel B).

Figure 2.11. Frequency of tax disputes and business attitude to dispute resolution

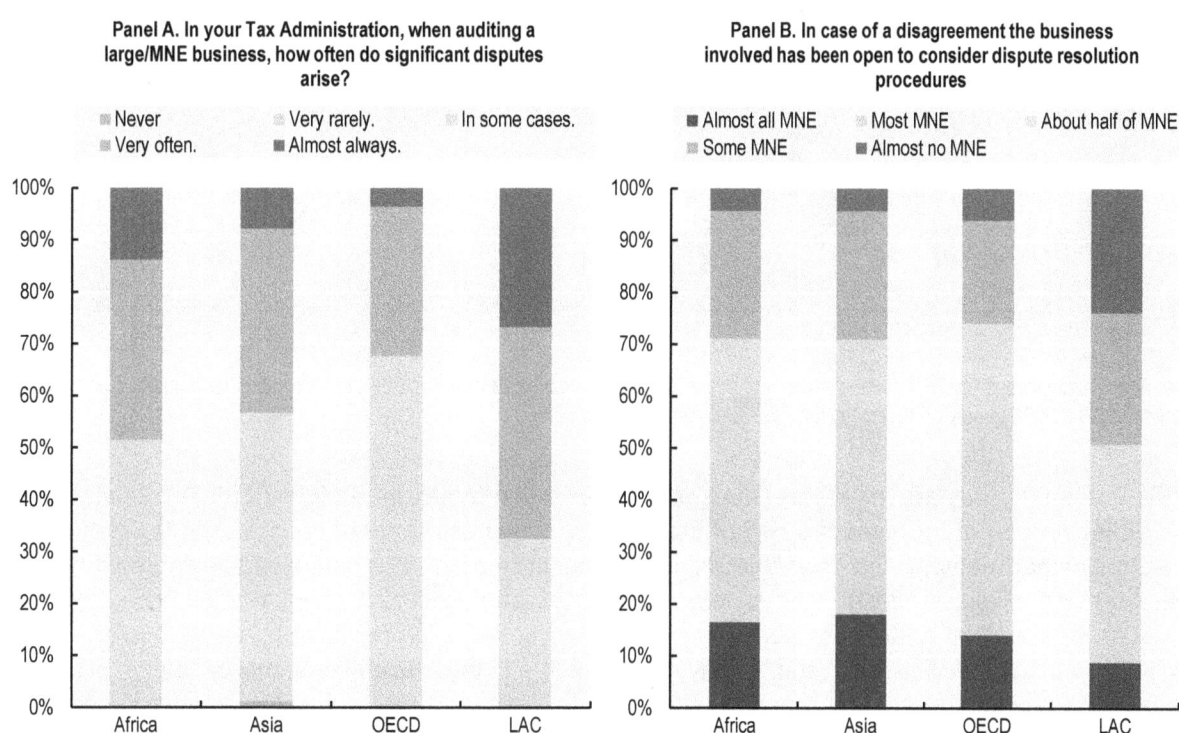

Note: Simple regional average. Countries are weighted so that no country represents more than 10% of their regional sample.
Source: OECD (2020), Survey on MNEs and Big Four Firms tax behaviour.

Tax officials generally consider large businesses/MNEs as being co-operative during dispute-resolution processes. Across regions, at least 70% of tax officials perceive large businesses/MNEs to be co-operative in all/most cases when seeking to resolve disputes. The best result is in Africa, where this number reaches 90% (Figure 2.12, Panel A). However, similar to the finding that a perception of co-operativeness is not a synonym for trust, being co-operative is not consistently interpreted as acting in good faith. In emerging regions, a much lower share of tax officials (between 50% and 70%) perceive large businesses/MNEs to act in good faith in all/most cases in the course of negotiations (Figure 2.12, Panel B).

Figure 2.12. Attitude of MNEs once a dispute resolution procedure has actually started

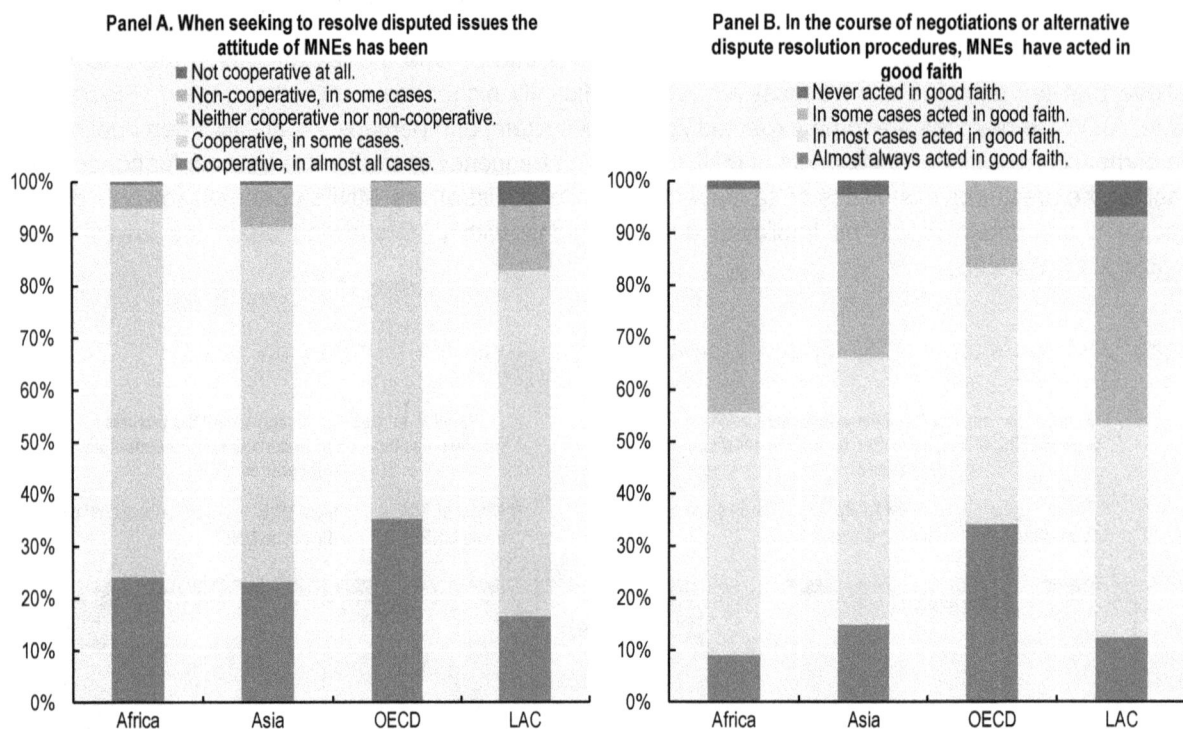

Panel A. When seeking to resolve disputed issues the attitude of MNEs has been
- Not cooperative at all.
- Non-cooperative, in some cases.
- Neither cooperative nor non-cooperative.
- Cooperative, in some cases.
- Cooperative, in almost all cases.

Panel B. In the course of negotiations or alternative dispute resolution procedures, MNEs have acted in good faith
- Never acted in good faith.
- In some cases acted in good faith.
- In most cases acted in good faith.
- Almost always acted in good faith.

Note: Simple regional average. Countries are weighted so that no country represents more than 10% of their regional sample.
Source: OECD (2020), Survey on MNEs and Big Four Firms tax behaviour.

While some disputes are inevitable, the approaches taken by tax administrations and businesses can either reduce or increase the risk of disputes. The aggressiveness of businesses tax planning is one of the primary determinants of whether disputes arise; businesses thus have a certain degree of control over the risk of disputes through their approach to tax risk (see (Bruhne, 2022[2]) and (Quentin, 2017[3])). However, as identified in the roundtables, amnesties may in some cases create perverse incentives that alter business risk calculations. Disputes may also arise due to legitimate differences of opinion over how the law is to be interpreted, though as Figure 2.3 showed, some businesses could be more co-operative in seeking to resolve misunderstandings and reduce the risk of disputes. Additionally, as discussed in the roundtables, disputes can also arise as a result of challenges with the processes in the tax system. While tax administrations may have little scope to reduce disputes originating from aggressive tax planning by MNEs, it is a shared interest of both businesses and tax administrations to reduce disputes caused by misunderstandings and processes.

Data from the MNE survey highlight several issues that may lead to disputes and reveal a strong desire by MNEs to improve dispute resolution. For instance, "unclear, poorly drafted tax legislation" was ranked as the greatest source of tax uncertainty in Africa, second in the OECD and eighth in Asia and Latin America. Meanwhile, unpredictable or inconsistent treatment by the tax authority was ranked as the primary source of tax uncertainty in Asia, second in the LAC region, third in Africa and sixth in the OECD. Complexity of the tax legislation was ranked the third-highest source of tax uncertainty in LAC and the OECD (twelfth and sixteenth in Asia and Africa respectively) while inconsistencies or conflicts between tax authorities on their interpretations of international tax standards was ranked third in Asia, fifth in Africa and LAC, and seventh in the OECD. Effective dispute resolution was seen as the most important tool for improving tax certainty in Asia and LAC, second in Africa and third in OECD.

The roundtables suggested there is scope for processes to prevent minor issues escalating into legal disputes. Participants highlighted that a high level of rigidity could lead to unnecessary disputes. For instance, small unintended errors from firms that could be resolved through communication and flexibility from the tax administration can result in a dispute. Businesses perceived that, in some jurisdictions, administrations take an (excessively) arbitrary an approach to audits (rather than basing these on risks); additional problems may arise in the absence of dispute-prevention mechanisms, such as channels to discuss disagreements and penalties without resorting to judicial appeals, increasing the likelihood of disagreements escalating to full-scale lawsuits. This lack of process can create confusion, especially where there is a lack of transparency on how any sanctions/penalties are decided or applied, and can give the impression that tax administrations are too aggressive or unfair. Some businesses also noted a challenge where litigation processes were lengthy, and sometimes/often followed by tax amnesties. This approach not only creates uncertainty but it also imposes costs on compliant taxpayers while effectively rewarding uncompliant ones, creating a perverse incentive structure.

2.6. Use of power and incentives

While most officials perceived that companies use their power legitimately, there are a significant minority of tax officials that perceive widespread abuse of power. The potential for large businesses/MNEs to abuse their economic and political power is a widespread concern. The survey results provide perceptions across several areas where such power could be abused: actions in negotiations; lobbying for, and use of, incentives; and staff recruitment. The results also provide perceptions on the legitimacy of the Big Four's use of power to lobby. These questions showed that while most tax officials see most large businesses/MNEs and the Big Four using their power legitimately, there is a large minority, especially in Africa and the LAC region, that perceive illegitimate behaviour. There was less discussion on these issues in the roundtables, as many participants highlighted that the opportunities for such abuse of power sat elsewhere (e.g. with ministries/politicians granting incentives). There is also limited information on MNE perceptions beyond the importance of tax incentives.

In all regions, a majority of tax officials perceive large businesses/MNEs acting legally and in good faith during most negotiations and dispute resolution, but by only a small margin in the LAC region and Africa. As highlighted in the previous section, while over three quarters of officials in OECD countries see good faith engagement in all or most cases, this falls to just 56% in Africa and 53% in the LAC region, suggesting there is significant scope for improvement (Figure 2.12, Panel B).

Improving domestic dispute resolution may provide an opportunity to reduce scope for abuse of power, as well as improving tax certainty for business. While businesses themselves have the primary obligation to ensure they are acting legally and in good faith, there may be scope for tax administrations to improve procedures, enhance the incentives for businesses to act in good faith, and reduce the scope to exert illegal influence. This demand for improved dispute resolution appears to be shared by MNEs, as effective dispute resolution is one of the top three tools requested by MNEs in all regions.

Perceptions of lobbying behaviour are fairly consistent, especially among tax officials in the OECD, Africa and Asia, with a majority perceiving limited and legitimate lobbying. Questions on lobbying covered large businesses' lobbying for tax incentives and the Big Four on both clients' individual cases, and tax policy more generally. Regarding the Big Four, tax officials in OECD countries were the least likely to see the Big Four as having no power to influence either individual cases or tax policies/laws, but most likely to view that power is used legitimately. In all regions, over 59% of officials saw the Big Four as having either no power, or using their power legitimately in both individual cases and tax policies/laws. Between 20-35% see the Big Four as sometimes using their power illegitimately, while a small minority see a frequent pattern of illegitimate behaviour (Figure 2.13, Panel B). Increased transparency by both authorities and the Big Four may help both build confidence that most interactions are legitimate, as well as reduce the scope and increase the accountability, for illegitimate interactions. In respect to large business/MNE lobbying to obtain tax incentives outside of existing legislation, perceptions are similar across the OECD, Africa and Asia, with around 60% of officials reporting no/some engagement in lobbying, this is much lower in the LAC region (43%). While around a quarter of tax officials in Africa, Asia and OECD see most/all businesses lobbying for specific incentives, this increases to 47% in the LAC region (Figure 2.13, Panel A).

Figure 2.13. Perceptions of lobbying behaviour

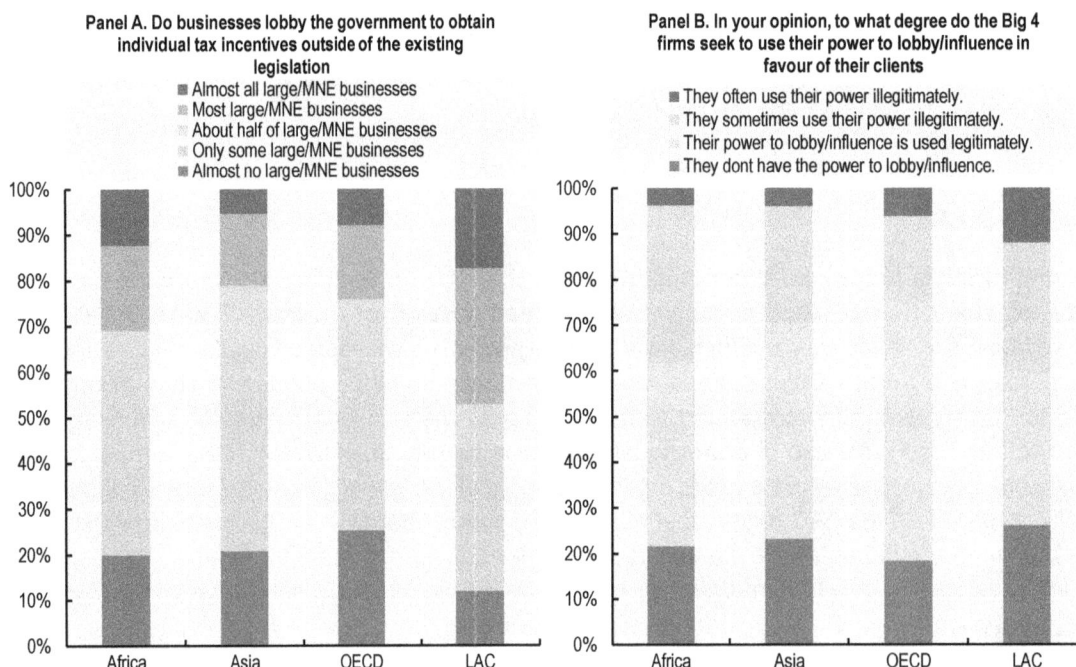

Panel A. Do businesses lobby the government to obtain individual tax incentives outside of the existing legislation

- Almost all large/MNE businesses
- Most large/MNE businesses
- About half of large/MNE businesses
- Only some large/MNE businesses
- Almost no large/MNE businesses

Panel B. In your opinion, to what degree do the Big 4 firms seek to use their power to lobby/influence in favour of their clients

- They often use their power illegitimately.
- They sometimes use their power illegitimately.
- Their power to lobby/influence is used legitimately.
- They dont have the power to lobby/influence.

Note: Simple regional average. Countries are weighted so that no country represents more than 10% of their regional sample.
Source: OECD (2020), Survey on MNEs and Big Four Firms tax behaviour.

Tax incentives for investment are much more widespread outside the OECD and more likely to be perceived as not being used as intended by legislation. Some 41% of tax officials in OECD countries responded that either no tax incentives were offered or tax incentives were offered to only a small extent, compared with around 10% in Asia and the LAC region, and 3% in Africa (Figure 2.14). Sector-specific incentives account for most of that difference: just 10% of OECD officials responded that tax incentives were only available for specific sectors, compared with around 36% in Africa and Asia, and 47% in the LAC region. Greater use of sector-specific incentives, which may create uncertainty over which firms are eligible for the incentive, may be part of the reason why businesses are more likely to be perceived as using incentives in a way not intended by legislation outside the OECD. While 70% of officials in the OECD say most or all businesses use incentives as intended, this drops to 59% in Asia, 51% in Africa and 48% in the LAC region.

Despite the widespread use of tax incentives outside the OECD, MNEs only identify tax incentives as one of the most important tax factors affecting investment location in the LAC region. Tax incentives were ranked 3rd most important out of 12 issues affecting investment in the LAC region, compared with 7th in Asia and 8th in Africa and OECD. The introduction of the global minimum tax as agreed by the Inclusive Framework as pillar two of the two pillar solution to addressing the tax challenges of the digitalising economy is likely to change perceptions concerning the value of tax incentives, and should help encourage the reform of tax incentives. The roundtables noted the importance of reforms to increase the transparency and accountability of tax incentives so as to reduce the opportunity for, and improve the identification of, illegitimate behaviour.

Figure 2.14. How often are tax incentives provided to large businesses/MNEs?

To what extent does your country provide tax incentives to large businesses/MNEs as a tool to attract investments?

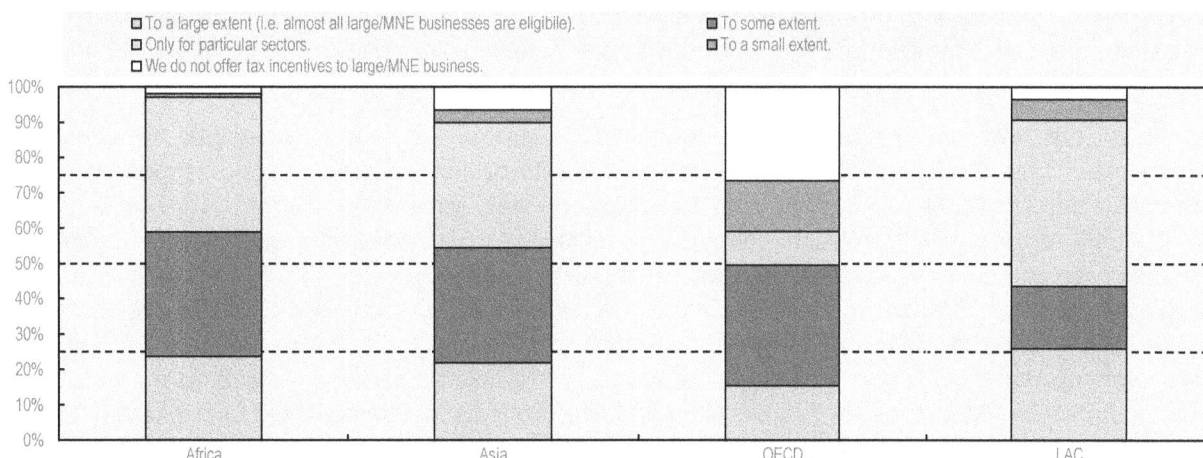

Note: Simple regional average. Countries are weighted so that no country represents more than 10% of their regional sample.
Source: OECD (2020), Survey on MNEs and Big Four Firms tax behaviour.

More than a quarter of African tax officials perceive that MNEs and/or the Big Four hire tax officials to directly influence ongoing tax disputes. Some 28% of African tax officials perceive this behaviour, substantially more than elsewhere (19% in the LAC region, 15% in Asia, 12% in the OECD) (Figure 2.15). This suggests that in Africa, especially, there is a need for new policies and processes, by both governments and by MNEs/the Big Four, to reduce this practice. Such measures could also seek to ensure that networks and contacts are not used illegitimately, as gaining access to the networks and contacts of public officials was seen as an important motivation for hiring public sector tax officials in all regions. While the use of such networks can be legitimate, safeguards are needed to ensure there is no impropriety.

Figure 2.15. Reasons why MNEs and/or the Big Four hire public officials

What are the main reasons why MNEs and/or the Big Four seek to hire public officials working on tax?

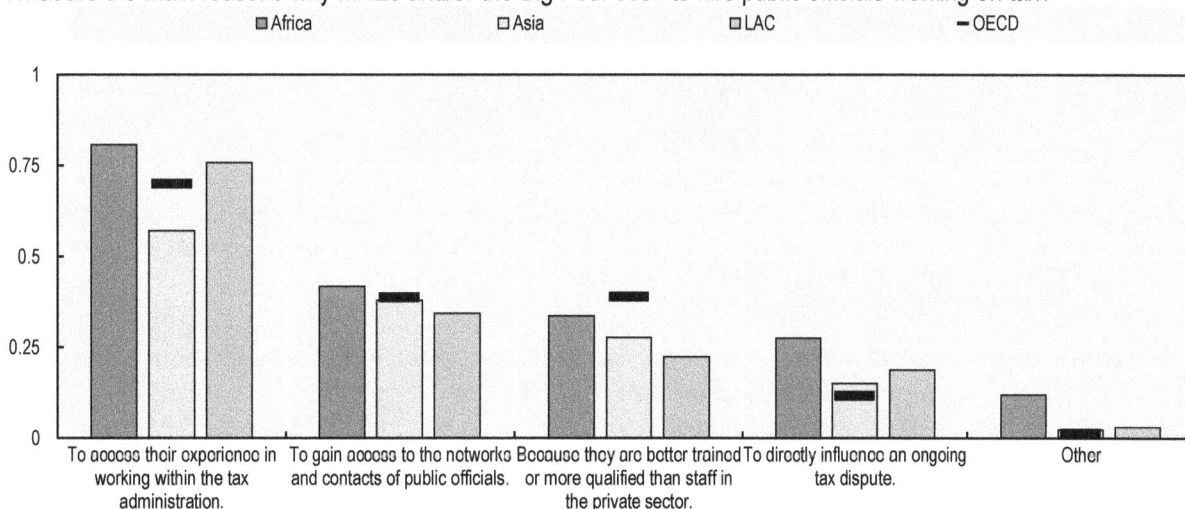

Note: Simple regional average. Countries are weighted so that no country represents more than 10% of their regional sample.
Source: OECD (2020), Survey on MNEs and Big Four Firms tax behaviour.

2.6.1. Bribery

A zero-tolerance policy towards bribery and a shared culture of integrity are essential to ensure fair implementation of the tax system. The interactions required between auditors and business and the complex application of tax laws in practice (which often involves a degree of discretion and interpretation) place revenue administrations at high risk of bribery attempts and corruption. The survey measured perceptions of bribery and corruption by asking tax officials to indicate the extent to which they agreed with the statement "Large/MNE business usually do not attempt to bribe tax officials in order to obtain beneficial outcomes".

A small but worrying percentage of respondents perceived bribery attempts as common. Responses to the bribery question must be interpreted with caution, as the number of respondents who decided not to answer or declared not to be aware varies widely across regions (from 34% in Asia to 55% in the LAC region), making regional comparisons difficult. Among those who did answer, a small but worrying percentage of respondents perceived bribery attempts as common: 15% of officials in Asia, 20% of officials in the LAC region, and 16% of officials in Africa view half or more of MNEs/large businesses as attempting to bribe tax officials. The proportion drops to 10% in OECD countries (Figure 2.16). OECD countries also have the highest percentage of any region of officials perceiving that almost no business attempts to bribe (81%). Despite its limitations, the data suggests that some large businesses/MNEs are attempting to bribe. This is a concern for all regions – including the OECD – in an area where there needs to be zero tolerance.

Figure 2.16. Perception of bribery by large businesses/MNE

Large/MNE business usually do not attempt to bribe tax officials in order to obtain beneficial outcomes

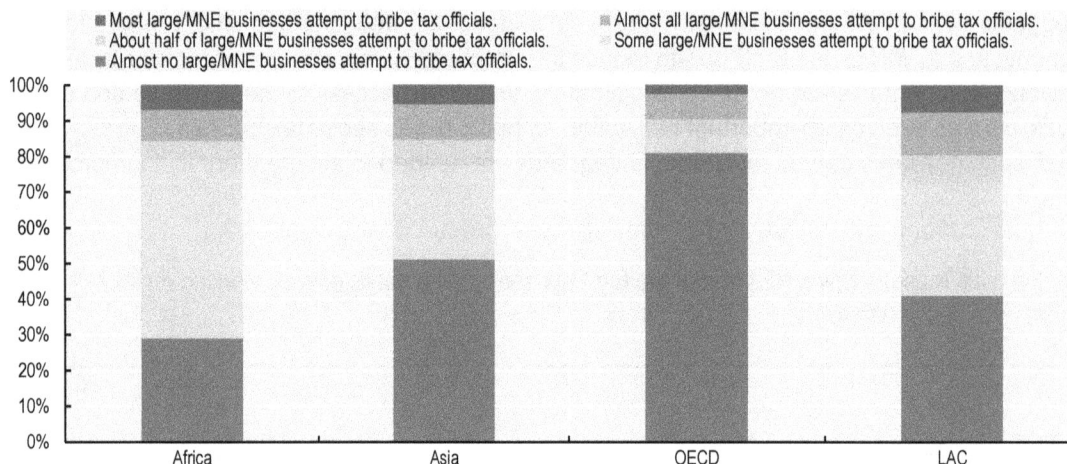

Note: Simple regional average. Countries are weighted so that no country represents more than 10% of their regional sample. Respondents who answered "I am not aware." were not included. For Africa they accounted for 49%, for Asia 34%, for LAC 55% and for the OECD 49%.
Source: OECD (2020), Survey on MNEs and Big Four Firms tax behaviour.

MNEs identify corruption as a major challenge, although corruption in the tax administration is less of a concern than corruption in the economy as a whole. Corruption is mentioned as a key factor for investment decisions in all regions, and is identified as the most important factor in the LAC region and Asia. In OECD countries, corruption was ranked as the 2nd most important factor affecting investment choices, while it was the 3rd factor of concern for MNEs in Africa. When asked specifically about the tax-related factors that influence their decisions, corruption in the tax system appears less important, MNEs operating in LAC ranked corruption in the tax system 6th out of 21 sources of tax uncertainty, above

Asia (13th), Africa (14th) and OECD countries (20th). MNEs therefore seem to perceive corruption as a bigger challenge in the LAC region whereas tax officials appear to view bribery as a bigger challenge in Asia, although this may in part be because officials in Asia are more willing to disclose their perceptions of bribery.

Participants in the roundtables reiterated the need for zero tolerance on bribery, and for concrete steps to reduce opportunities for corruption. The roundtables highlighted the benefits of digitalisation in reducing the scope for bribery, as well as the need for effective oversight. Absence of audit and risk committees, as well as countries not having layered dispute resolution processes, were also identified as creating scope for bribery, especially of auditors. The roundtable discussions recognised a tension between facilitating increased and more informal interactions between taxpayers and tax administrations, and the increased opportunity for bribery/illegitimate behaviour that these might create. Various approaches to reduce risks were shared, including regular staff rotations (while ensuring continuity and certainty for taxpayers), the need for multiple staff to be present at all meetings, and keeping records of interactions with taxpayers. Administrations also stressed the importance of promoting a culture of public integrity.

The roundtables also highlighted the impact of perceived corruption on tax morale. One speaker highlighted the wide body of evidence showing that perceptions of corruption are a key factor affecting tax morale. Research shows that low perceptions of corruption at different levels of the executive branch (president's office, government officials, or tax authorities) have a significant and positive impact on tax revenues (Boly, Konte and Shimeles, 2020[4]). Fighting corruption (or eliminating it altogether) also has a significant and negative impact on the share of income evaded, suggesting spillover effects from anticorruption to tax morale (Banerjee, Roly and Gillanders, 2020[5]). This matches findings in the 2019 OECD report on tax morale (OECD, 2019[6]).

2.7. Staff recruitment

While movement of staff between the tax administration and the private sector is relatively limited on average, turnover can be very high in some cases. At least 75% of tax administrations in all regions reported that 20% or less of staff have been lost to the private sector in the last five years (Figure 2.17), and almost 90% in all regions report less than 20% of staff were lost to the Big Four in the same period. However, some officials report extremely high levels of loss to the private sector; it is especially concerning that in Africa, the region where tax administrations have the lowest capacity, 2% of officials report that over 60% of staff have been lost to the private sector in five years, a higher share than any other region. In terms of recruitment from the private sector, it appears that tax administrations in LAC are the most likely to recruit from the private sector, with 26% of officials reporting 20% or more staff were recruited from the private sector in the last five years, over 10 percentage points more than any other region.

Figure 2.17. How often do public officials go to work for the private sector and vice versa?

In the past 5 years in your team, what percentage of staff has been lost to the private sector and how many have been recruited from the private sector?

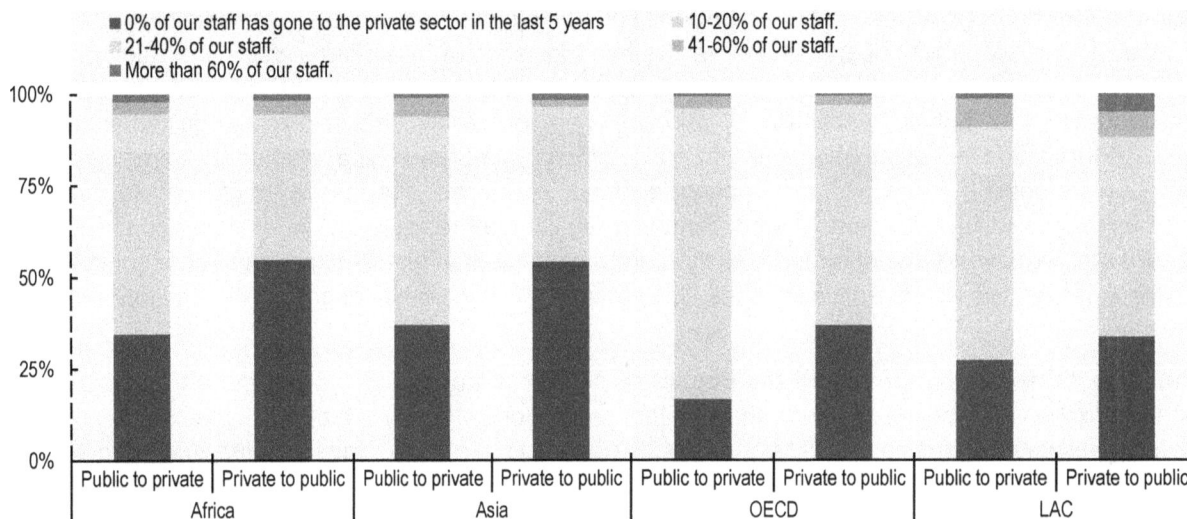

Note: Simple regional average. Countries are weighted so that no country represents more than 10% of their regional sample. Public to private refers to the percentage of staff has been lost to the private sector? Private to public refers to the percentage of staff recruited from the private sector.
Source: OECD (2020), Survey on MNEs and Big Four Firms tax behaviour.

The private sector is perceived to recruit tax administration staff primarily for their experience. That tax administration officials are recruited for their experience of working within the tax administration is unsurprising. However, it is notable that while at least 70% of officials in Africa, OECD and LAC countries cite this factor, only 57% of Asian officials do. A much lower share believes tax administration staff are recruited by the private sector because they are better trained and/or qualified than other staff in the private sector (see Figure 2.15). This view is most common among OECD tax administrators, suggesting that the capacity gap between the private and public sectors may be greater outside the OECD. Reducing the value of experience of working within the tax administration may help reduce loss of staff to the private sector, in countries where this is a problem. For example, increasing the transparency of tax administration functioning may help in this regard.

Lack of experienced staff in tax administrations is a significant concern for MNEs, suggesting a shared interest in ensuring tax administrations are able to retain staff. MNEs cited lack of expertise in tax administrations on international taxation as one of the leading sources of tax uncertainty (6th out of 21 sources in Africa, 9th in Asia, 10th in the LAC region and 13th in OECD countries), highlighting that retaining experienced staff is a shared priority for tax administrations and the private sector. While challenges in staff retention are not solely due to staff leaving for the private sector (for example, this might arise from routine staff rotation in many administrations), it can be a contributory factor. This shared interest among the public and private sector may make it easier to develop processes and procedures to regulate the movement of staff between the two. Such movement should not be stopped entirely, as there are mutual benefits to enabling relevant skills and experience to flow in both directions. However, it would be beneficial to establish clear guidelines and boundaries to regulate this movement, especially where turnover is very high and/or where there are concerns about illegitimate behaviour (see Use of power and incentives).

2.8. Comparison with local businesses

The survey asked for perceptions of the behaviour of MNEs and the Big Four relative to that of local businesses. To help contextualise the results and address the risk that the difference between perceived behaviour of local and foreign businesses may skew the results, the survey asked officials about their perception of local businesses in comparison to MNEs, and about local advisory firms in comparison to the Big Four. These results were not discussed in detail during the roundtables, and there is not relevant data from the MNE tax certainty survey to provide additional context.

The most common view in all regions was that compliance is similar between local businesses and MNEs. Where a difference was perceived officials were more likely to view MNEs as more compliant than local businesses. In Africa and Asia, almost 50% of officials see compliance as equal between local businesses and MNEs, this was slightly lower in LAC, and lowest in the OECD. The officials from the OECD were most likely to see local businesses as less compliant than MNEs, with 40% expressing that view, although all regions were in the range of 30%-40%. The range that saw local businesses as more compliant was also fairly narrow, ranging from 13% in Asia to 24% in the LAC region (Figure 2.18).

These results suggest that improving tax morale is at least equally important in domestic businesses. Given that MNEs are more likely to be seen as compliant, there may be a role for MNEs to show leadership in encouraging compliance, including through their value chains.

Figure 2.18. Are local businesses more compliant than large/MNE business?

In terms of their tax behaviour, do you think that local businesses, in comparison to MNEs are?

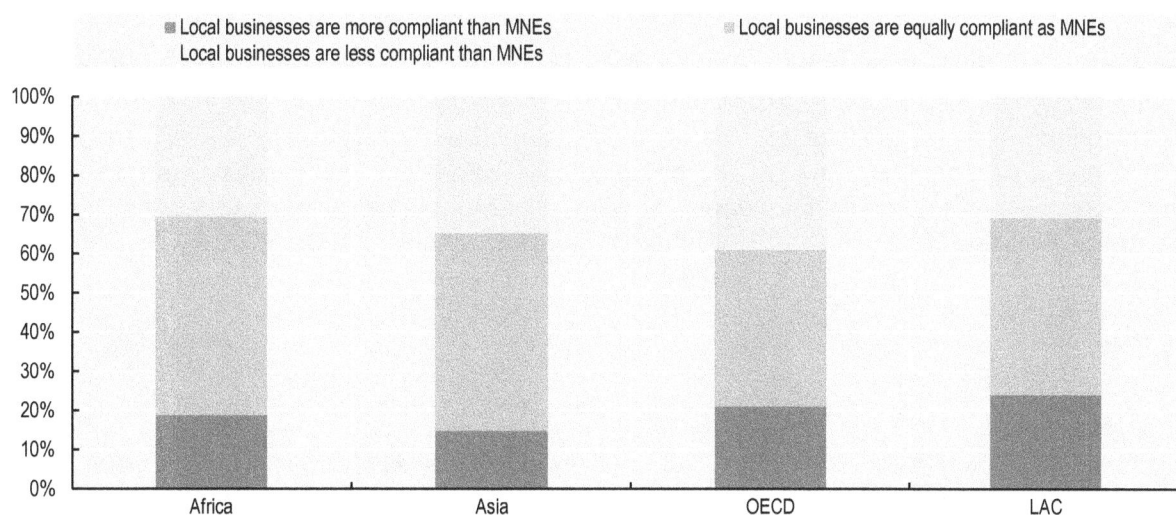

Note: Simple regional average. Countries are weighted so that no country represents more than 10% of their regional sample.
Source: OECD (2020), Survey on MNEs and Big Four Firms tax behaviour.

Officials in all regions were more likely to perceive the Big Four as advising their clients to be more aggressive in their tax strategies than local advisors. In Africa, Asia and the OECD, 42%-45% of officials viewed the Big Four as advising clients to be more aggressive than local firms; this figure rose to nearly 60% in the LAC region. The proportion of officials perceiving the Big Four to advise clients to be less aggressive was highest in Asia, at 24%, and lowest in the LAC region at 12% (Figure 2.19, Panel A)

Figure 2.19. Influence of the Big Four on their clients' tax behaviour

Panel A. In comparison to local tax advisors, do you think that the Big 4 firms:

- Advise to be more aggressive in their tax strategies
- No influence
- To be less aggressive

Panel B. Do the activities and advice of the Big 4 encourage their clients to?

- Be less compliant
- Have no impact on compliance
- Be more compliant

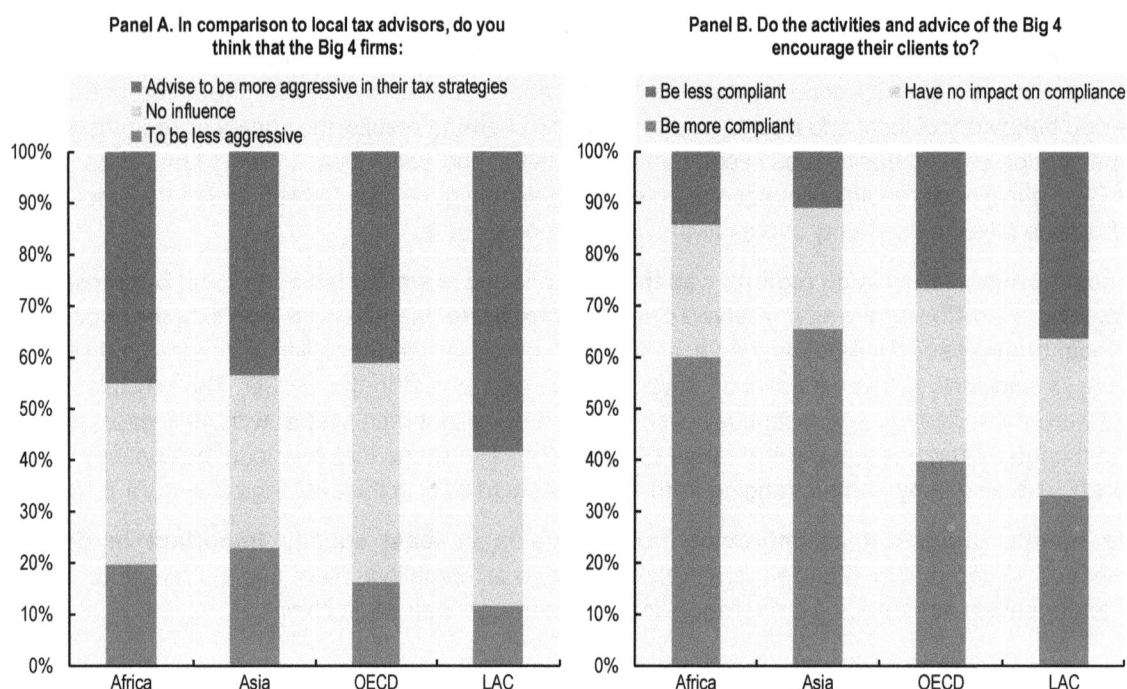

Note: Simple regional average. Countries are weighted so that no country represents more than 10% of their regional sample.
Source: OECD (2020), Survey on MNEs and Big Four Firms tax behaviour.

The Big Four are more likely to be perceived as encouraging their clients to be more compliant and willing to pay tax, except in the LAC region. This was most apparent in Africa and Asia, where around 60% of officials view the Big Four as encouraging compliance and willingness to pay tax (compared to 40% in the OECD and 33% in the LAC region) (Figure 2.19, Panel B). This regional difference may, at least in part, be a reflection of the tax morale of the populations as a whole, as previous research identified tax morale as being lower in Africa and Asia than in the OECD and LAC (OECD, 2019[6]).

References

Banerjee, R., A. Roly and R. Gillanders (2020), *Anti-tax evasion, anti-corruption and public good provision: an experimental analysis of policy spillovers*, https://doi.org/10.2139/ssrn.3652411. [5]

Boly, A., M. Konte and A. Shimeles (2020), *Corruption and Tax Morale in Africa, Working Paper Series N° 333*, African Development Bank, https://www.afdb.org/fr/documents/working-paper-333-corruption-and-tax-morale-africa. [4]

Bruhne, A. (2022), *Defining and Managing Corporate Tax Risk: Perceptions of Tax Risk Experts*, https://doi.org/10.1111/1911-3846.12785. [2]

OECD (2021), *Developing Countries and the OECD/G20 Inclusive Framework om BEPS: OECD Report for the G20 Finance Ministers and Central Bank Governors, October 2021, Italy*, OECD, https://www.oecd.org/tax/beps/developing-countries-and-the-oecd-g20-inclusive-framework-on-beps.htm. [1]

OECD (2019), *Tax Morale: What Drives People and Businesses to Pay Tax?*, OECD Publishing, [6] https://doi.org/10.1787/f3d8ea10-en.

Quentin (2017), "Risk-Mining the public Exchequer", *Journal of Tax Administration*, Vol. 3/2, [3] pp. 22-35, http://jota.website/index.php/JoTA/article/view/142/118.

3 Building trust, improving transparency and communication

This chapter provides a range of actions to help build trust and improve transparency and communication between tax administrations and taxpayers. These cover both existing good practices and new ideas suggested by participants in the roundtable discussions.

The survey results clearly indicate a need to build trust between tax administrations and business, while the roundtables discussions demonstrated a willingness from both tax administrations and businesses to improve the relationships and enhance trust between large taxpayers/advisors and tax administrations.

Trust was the focus of much of the discussions at the roundtables, and was identified as integral in other areas, including transparency and communication. 'Trust' in this case should be seen as having trust in the processes, and that all parties are engaging in good faith. Tax is complex, and there will be disagreements, especially in international tax issues. While improving the relationships between taxpayers and administrations should reduce disputes, it will not eliminate them. Improved trust, however, should enable disputes to be resolved, with all parties accepting the validity of differing positions and (crucially) the results of a resolution process, without it affecting the willingness of either side to maintain a positive relationship.

Building trust is neither quick nor simple, there is no single solution; nor can trust be built by one party alone. Building trust requires commitments and action from both taxpayers and tax administrations. While the overall objective is to improve the tax morale of taxpayers, it is necessary to look at measures that can be taken by all parties, as there are a range of factors that may affect tax morale. Growing interest among investors, the media, civil society organisations and the public more generally in the tax affairs of large businesses indicates that a wider set of actors may play a role. The specific measures that these other actors can take are, however, outside of the scope of this report.

This section highlights best practices and recommendations that came from the regional roundtables, as well as identifying some areas for further work. These have been grouped together in four clusters; while not entirely mutually exclusive (for example there is/can be a capacity building element to all clusters), these clusters illustrate the different dimensions that need to be considered in building trust between tax administrations and business. The clusters are:

- Compliance and Audit strategies
- Expectations and accountability of behaviour
- Transparency and communication
- Capacity building

The measures range from those that are relatively easy to implement, to more comprehensive reforms that may require substantial resources. Especially where resources, both human and financial, are limited, as they are in many tax administrations and businesses, securing agreement to invest the time and resources can be challenging. The potential return on investment in these measures is significant: however, the challenge may be that some of the investments required may not be so familiar, with a focus less on technical processes or skills, but rather professional competences that can build trust and mutual understanding.

While these measures may imply an increased resource commitment for tax administrations to begin with, costs savings should be realised in the medium- and long-term. Over time, improving trust, communications and transparency with taxpayers should lead to cost savings. Stronger relationships will enable better prioritisation of resources, not least through better targeting of audits, which will reduce case-handling time and disputes.

From the business perspective, the potential gains in tax certainty will be of clear benefit. In addition, with tax increasingly a concern for shareholders, especially those applying ESG criteria, an increasing number of MNEs should be able to make an additional case for such investment in measures to increase trust, communications, and transparency.

The largest barrier to committing to approaches that focus on building trust, improving communication, and increasing transparency may be uncertainty regarding whether efforts will be

reciprocated. Given that taxpayers and tax administrations stand to benefit, there are clearly good reasons for reciprocity, but change can take time. As such, new approaches should not be viewed as a short-term project, and while results may appear quickly, they should not be expected immediately. In addition, communicating clearly about changes and the expectations accompanying these changes is likely to encourage reciprocal responses, while seeking and acting on feedback will accelerate the process. Developing a clear strategy, with commitment from senior officials, on how to build trust, will therefore be useful. This may entail a comprehensive co-operative compliance approach, but could be more modest to start with.

3.1. Compliance and audit strategies

Creating an environment that encourages compliance is important. While the right strategies can build trust, those that are poorly designed and/or executed can inhibit trust and reduce the willingness to engage openly. The roundtables identified a number of strategic approaches that can build trust and encourage dialogue.

3.1.1. Co-operative compliance

The term 'co-operative compliance' refers to approaches that provide a framework to establish a relationship with taxpayers based on co-operation and trust (OECD, 2016[1]). This approach is distinct from a coercive or obligation-based relationship. The concept not only describes the process of co-operation but also demonstrates its goal as part of the revenue body's compliance risk management strategy: compliance that leads to payment of the right amount of tax at the right time. In dealings with taxpayers, co-operative compliance entails revenue bodies demonstrating understanding based on commercial awareness, impartiality, proportionality, openness through disclosure and transparency, and responsiveness. In return, taxpayers provide disclosure and transparency in their dealings with revenue bodies.

Co-operative compliance was considered desirable in all the roundtables, especially by businesses. In some instances, co-operative compliance was referred to as an enhanced relationship between taxpayer and tax administration. It was noted in the discussions that co-operative compliance may be more appropriately seen as an end point rather than a departure point, as a certain degree of trust needs to be established to enable a comprehensive co-operative compliance framework. This may explain why MNEs identified establishing co-operative compliance programmes as a low priority among the tools to improve tax certainty (between 19th and 21st out of 25 possible measures across all regions).

Co-operative compliance can be a resource-intensive undertaking, but should be resource-efficient in the long run. It may be challenging for developing countries with weak capacity to implement co-operative compliance, at least in full. For example, it may be challenging within existing capacities to manage the 'real time' dialogue envisaged in co-operative compliance. In addition, where trust is limited, it may not be possible to move directly to co-operative compliance, even if resources were available: although co-operative compliance can build trust, it requires a certain level of trust to begin with. There were, therefore, discussions about what co-operative compliance 'lite' could look like, which focused on the key starting points for countries and businesses seeking to move towards co-operative compliance.

Building an effective co-operative compliance system requires commitment and actions from both taxpayers and tax administrations. Without taxpayers and tax administrations committing to the approach, co-operative compliance will fail. For example, if taxpayers do not commit to the implementation of Tax Control Frameworks (TCFs – see Tax Control Frameworks section below), there is a risk that tax administrations will invest heavily in enhanced services to taxpayers without receiving the amount of information and degree of co-operation from taxpayers that would justify this investment.

Many developing countries appear to be moving towards the co-operative compliance approach. Fifty-three of the 101 developing countries participating in the ISORA[1] survey state that a co-operative compliance programme is available for large taxpayers (see Box 3.1 for examples from Latin America). There may, however, be differences in interpretation as to what entails co-operative compliance, with research showing that there is significant variation in the requirements and processes in countries that report co-operative compliance regimes (see (Martini, 2022[2])). While co-operative compliance is likely to vary between countries, not least due to legal and structural differences, too great a variety in approaches labelled co-operative compliance may generate confusion among taxpayers and tax administrations alike. The WU Global Tax Policy Center, together with the International Chamber of Commerce and Commonwealth Association of Tax Administrators, has developed a handbook on co-operative compliance that identifies and explains key elements of successful co-operative compliance programmes (Owens, 2021[3]). Similarly, several of the best practices identified by the roundtables, and summarised in this report, could be components of a co-operative compliance framework.

Box 3.1. Co-operative compliance in Latin America

According to the ISORA data a third of countries in the LAC region state that co-operative compliance is available to large taxpayers. Two countries that provided examples in the LAC roundtable were Chile and Colombia.

Chile

Chile's *Servicio de* Impuestos Internos (SII) promotes co-operative compliance through two main tools:

1. Collaboration Agreements for Tax Compliance (ACCT) – currently in a pilot phase. Participating MNEs benefit from opportunities to discuss and regularise any disagreement with the tax administration before an audit process is opened against them or before any fines or penalties are imposed. If inconsistencies are detected during the information cross-checking and validation processes, analysis and conversation with the taxpayer are initiated in the first instance. It is expected that these will serve to correct any discrepancy; only if this does not occur is the action escalated to an audit.

   MNEs wishing to enter into these agreements are required to have in place a solid corporate tax governance structure and an internal fiscal control framework that guarantees that the tax returns and information submitted to the tax administration are complete and correct. Such Tax Control Frameworks (TCF - see below) are a key feature of co-operative compliance and help build trust.

2. Collaboration Agreements (ACT) with sectorial or trade associations of taxpayers of different sizes (large, medium and small companies), which to leverage these associations to encourage tax compliance. The tax administration develops a Work Plan of preventive and collaborative actions to reduce tax compliance gaps and mitigate risks with taxpayers belonging to the association. Work Plans include actions such as:

   o Workshops on tax issues of interest to the association;

   o Field visits and workshops held by the associations to allow SII officials to learn about the business and industry model that the association represents;

   o Special attention units to resolve remotely any doubts about tax declarations;

   o Workshops with members who present gaps in compliance to seek collaborative solutions;

   o On-site assistance to taxpayers;

   o Working groups between the association and the SII; and

○ Production of guidelines and support material on topics of interest.

Additionally, on a periodic basis, the SII team responsible for overseeing the implementation of the Agreement reviews the tax compliance status of its members with the association in each of the four categories of tax obligations (register, report, declare and pay).

This type of collaborative work opens a direct channel for associations with the SII to receive support and training on tax issues, answer tax inquiries or resolve doubts regarding common problems of their members. It also allows associations to receive personalised reports with the main gaps to be corrected, to detect risks and non-compliance, and to seek collaborative solutions.

Since 2017, Chile has signed 51 Agreements with trade associations, and it has established indicators for the explicit and objective evaluation of the results of this compliance programme (such as tracking the completion of activities included in the Working Plans, conducting qualitative evaluations and analysing the evolution of tax compliance gaps among members). These evaluations show that, on average, these taxpayers display better tax compliance rates than taxpayers not included in an ACT.

Colombia

Colombia's Dirección de Impuestos y Aduanas Nacionales (DIAN) promotes co-operative compliance through several different initiatives. All the initiatives listed below follow three key principles to ensure co-operative compliance programmes are fair, efficient and transparent: i) programmes are based on a legal framework that establishes the steps and procedures that regulate their application, eliminating the margin of discretion; ii) tax penalties are applied in the same way for all taxpayers, regardless of whether they participate in a cooperative compliance programme; and iii) the programmes establish indicators for the explicit and objective evaluation of the results of the compliance.

- Advanced Pricing Agreements (APAs) – APAs are agreements between the taxpayer and tax administration determining the transfer pricing methodology to be used, providing certainty for the duration of the agreement (so long as the terms and conditions are adhered to).

- 'Account Executives': tax administration officials with knowledge of DIAN processes provide large taxpayers with personalised attention regarding the services offered by the tax administration. The assistance is provided remotely, if possible, in order to eliminate barriers such as distance/location or the hours of reception of requests. They provide assistance in procedures related to internal and international tax, customs and foreign trade; provide responses and follow-up to petitions, complaints and claims; link them with other agencies or departments when necessary; and generate warnings and early alerts for taxpayers.

- Personalised communications informing taxpayers in advance of the expiration dates of their obligations or of the inconsistencies found in them, in order to allow them to regularise their situation before taking a decision on further measures and avoiding future litigation.

- Roundtables with unions or professional interest groups, in which the tax authorities explain common inconsistencies that appear in tax audits. They seek rapprochement between the administration and large taxpayers by highlighting that the tax administration has noticed the tax planning practices frequently found in the audit of the tax returns filed.

- Tax queries: taxpayers can request tax authorities to issue interpretations on tax matters. The interpretation must be followed by officials assigned to the entity, providing tax certainty.

Source: Inter-American Center of Tax Administrations (CIAT)

3.1.2. Risk-based approaches to audit

Both businesses and tax authorities participating in the roundtables highlighted the benefits of taking and/or improving risk-based approaches to audit. For tax administrations the benefits include improving the efficiency and effectiveness of audits, enabling limited resources to be used more effectively, while for taxpayers it can reduce compliance costs for low-risk taxpayers.

Risk-based audit strategies may also provide indirect benefits by influencing taxpayers' approach to compliance. When risk-based approaches are in place, companies are likely to be incentivised to reduce risky behaviour and improve internal control procedures to reduce risk; conversely, when risk-based approaches are absent, the appetite for tax risk increases, not least as there would be no guarantees that adopting a low tax risk would increase tax certainty. A study of 15 514 firms across 54 countries found that the use of risk-based audits is associated with a lower level of tax avoidance. The same research also found that the use of risk-based audits decreased the cost of enforcement and improved the performance of tax authorities (Eberhartinger, 2021[4])

While risk-based approaches to audit may reduce the cost of enforcement in the long run, establishing such approaches may increase resourcing needs in the short term, creating a challenge for some developing countries. There are increasingly sophisticated tools available to help analyse data to assess risk, which can be resource intensive to design. Tax administrations therefore need to establish systems of risk analysis that are tailored to the precision and sophistication of the resources (both human and financial) available, remembering that absolute precision is not the aim since that is the objective of the audit itself. Such an approach will need to establish key risk indicators, of which there may be several types (e.g. indicators reflecting general tax risk of different taxpayer groups, indicators relating to taxpayers' past behaviour, indicators relating to deviations of current performance from norms, and information from informants). CIAT has developed the *Manual on Non-Compliance Risk Management for Tax Administrations* (CIAT, 2020[5]) to guide tax administrations in their risk-management approaches.

The development of risk-based approaches can help with other challenges identified in the roundtables, especially issues around the volume of information requested. By focusing on key risks in both the initial filing requirements and any subsequent requests for additional information, the information demands should become smaller but more targeted, making it easier for tax administrations to carry out analysis and for taxpayers to comply. It should be noted that risk-based approaches create new challenges regarding information. It is necessary to ensure that the information used for risk analysis can be trusted and is not subject to bias; this may require investment in the tools to clean and sort data, especially when automated algorithms are used.

While risk-based approaches can help administrations make more effective use of data, they do not eliminate the need for dialogue beyond data exchanges. Sometimes there are differences in interpretation between tax administrations and taxpayers, but a risk-based approach can provide a structure for dialogue and ensure that it focuses on the most pertinent issues.

Tax administrations adopting risk-based approaches have to decide how much information to share regarding their approach. Transparency can be an effective tool to encourage specific changes in taxpayer behaviour and can build trust However, if too much information is shared, it could encourage clustering of behaviour just below thresholds. There is also scope for tax administrations to share information between themselves to help identify risks. For example, CIAT has established a *Database of Transnational Cases Involving the Erosion of the Taxable Base* to facilitate exchange between CIAT member countries on abusive tax planning.

3.2. Expectations/accountability of behaviour

There was strong agreement across participants in the roundtables that it is easier to build relationships when there are clear expectations for behaviour, and even more so where there is some form of accountability. This applies to taxpayers and tax administrations alike, although the mechanisms will differ. In addition, discussions on reducing scope for bribery and illegitimate behaviour also focussed on the need for accountability.

Administrations, taxpayers and advisors should all consider how objectives and performance targets affect relationships. Some businesses raised concerns that evaluating an auditor's performance based solely/primarily on their achievement of certain tax assessment targets could be detrimental to building trust, as it may promote more aggressive approaches to audit from the administration. Similarly, businesses and advisors should also consider whether their policies could be incentivising an overly aggressive approach. One suggestion in the roundtable was that investors evaluate a company's performance based on its pre-tax earnings, in order to avoid incentivising tax minimisation strategies.

While beyond the scope of this report, it should also be noted that ESG reporting increasingly includes reporting on tax. Tax is included in certain ESG reporting standards, such as the Global Reporting Initiative and the World Economic Forum International Business Council ESG reporting metrics. While adhering to such standards is voluntary, businesses are increasingly expected to align their tax behaviour accordingly (especially public disclosures), compliance with these standards is increasingly required for those businesses that wish to be included in ESG investment portfolios.

3.2.1. Guidelines

The existence of guidelines for large businesses correlates with an increased perception of trust in large taxpayers. Where such guidelines exist, taxpayers are generally perceived to follow them, suggesting they are effective in setting expectations for behaviour. MNEs also see guidance as a high priority for increasing tax certainty (see Chapter Two). When preparing new guidelines, care must be taken to ensure that they are sufficiently detailed; some businesses highlighted challenges where guidelines are not sufficiently detailed, since this can lead to unpredictable interpretation and an unclear decision-making process.

It is important to ensure widespread awareness of guidelines. As outlined in Chapter Two, some tax officials perceive that the guidelines that exist are never used, and there is some evidence to suggest differing levels of awareness of the existence of guidelines across tax officials within the same administration. Thus, internal awareness raising is also needed in addition to ensuring that taxpayers are aware of guidelines.

The OECD Guidelines for Multinational Enterprises (OECD, 2011[6]) **provide internationally agreed guidelines for MNEs operating in or from adhering countries, together with a network of National Contact Points (NCPs) to resolve issues related to the implementation of the Guidelines.** These Guidelines are the only multilaterally agreed and comprehensive code of responsible business conduct that governments have committed to promoting, and include a chapter on taxation. The taxation chapter states that MNEs should comply with both the letter and spirit of tax laws in the countries in which they operate. It also highlights the need for MNE boards to adopt tax risk-management strategies. NCPs provide for a non-judicial grievance process that allows any individual or organisation with a legitimate interest to submit a case to an NCP regarding an MNE operating in or from the country of the NCP that has not observed the guidelines. At the time of writing, there have been 18 cases brought under the taxation chapter of the MNE Guidelines.

3.2.2. Taxpayers' charters and ombudsmen

Taxpayers' charters provide clear expectations of service for taxpayers, while a tax ombudsman service plays a useful role in resolving procedural and administrative issues. Many countries have established taxpayers' charters, which provide a reference point for the standards of administrative service taxpayers can expect. Such charters outline the rights and obligations of taxpayers and explain what to expect when dealing with the tax administration. The perception of several businesses participating in the roundtables was that the value of such charters lies in improving the training and internal governance of tax administrations, rather than as a reference point for specific instances where it is felt that the charter is not being adhered to.

Even with taxpayers' charters, difficulties may arise with the administrative actions of the tax office. In these circumstances, the ability to refer to a tax ombudsman can resolve issues quickly and rebuild trust. A tax ombudsman is independent from a tax administration and will usually accept complaints only after a tax administration's internal complaints procedure has been exhausted. In most cases, the findings and/or directives of the ombudsman will be binding upon the tax authority, and as such referral to the ombudsman can be a quicker and cheaper process than recourse to the courts. In addition to playing a valuable role in resolving individual cases, an ombudsman can identify systemic or emerging issues to be highlighted to the tax authorities. The roundtables identified a tax ombudsman as a valuable institution for maintaining and rebuilding trust between tax authorities and taxpayers, and they identified a number of essential features for an effective tax ombudsman (see Box 3.2).

While a tax ombudsman focuses on the tax administration functions, clear expectations on legal processes are also required. This issue was not widely discussed in the roundtables, as it goes beyond the control of the tax administrations, but it is a significant concern. Unpredictable or inconsistent treatment by the courts was the 5th highest source of tax uncertainty in Asia and 7th in LAC (11th in Africa and 12th in the OECD). Countries may need to identify ways to provide assurances concerning treatment by the legal system, for example on provisions to ensure General Anti-Avoidance Rules will be applied objectively, such as the use of panels of experts and providing transparency on cases.

Box 3.2. Key design features of a tax ombudsman

A number of key features for an effective tax ombudsman were identified in the roundtable discussions, these include:

- The ombudsman should be established through legislation that specifies its mandate, limits on authority, access to information and obligation to maintain taxpayer confidentiality
- The ombudsman must be independent from the tax authorities
- The scope of matters to be dealt with by the ombudsman must be clearly defined and limited – i.e. they should be related to the service received from the tax authorities or should be of procedural or administrative nature
- Taxpayers should exhaust internal remedies first before referring to the ombudsman to avoid bypassing the processes of tax authorities
- The ombudsman must have access to information from the tax authority
- The ombudsman's findings/directives should be binding on the tax authorities
- The ombudsman should report periodically to the tax authorities, as well as to the oversight body (e.g. minister of finance/parliament)
- The ombudsman should keep the public informed as to its function and availability
- The ombudsman service should be accessible to all taxpayers (i.e. free to use)

Source: Summary of inputs from roundtable participants

3.2.3. Tax control frameworks

Tax control frameworks (TCF) have evolved alongside co-operative compliance, and in many countries, taxpayers are required to have a TCF in place as a condition of entry to a co-operative compliance programme. A TCF is the part of the system of internal control that assures the accuracy and completeness of the tax returns and disclosures made by an enterprise. Its importance lies in its ability to provide a verifiable assurance that the information and returns submitted by a taxpayer are both accurate and complete. This goes above and beyond the obligation to provide accurate tax returns, by placing additional emphasis on disclosure and transparency. In this respect, disclosure signifies the willingness of the taxpayer to make the revenue body aware of any tax positions taken in the return that may be uncertain or controversial, and being ready to go beyond their statutory obligations to disclose, while transparency refers to the sharing sufficient information about the taxpayer's internal control system to enable the tax administration to justify trust in the taxpayer. In this respect, the TCF may be a useful part of the risk analysis (see risk-based approaches to audit). In many cases, a TCF will be a part of the broader business control framework of an enterprise.

The 2016 publication *Co-operative Tax Compliance: Building Better Tax Control Frameworks* (OECD, 2016[1]) outlines the six essential features of TCFs. They are: that a tax strategy is established and owned by the senior management of the enterprise; it is applied comprehensively, such that all transactions capable of affecting the tax position are covered by the TCF; responsibility should be clearly assigned, with the board ultimately accountable, while the tax department is responsible (and resourced) for implementation; the governance of the TCF needs to be such that it ensures that not only are all relevant transactions and events reviewed, but also documented; there should also be regular monitoring and testing of the TCF. Taken together, the first five of these features should enable the sixth to be fulfilled; providing assurance that tax risks are subject to proper control. The exact design and implementation of TCFs will vary between enterprises, especially across sectors.

An increasing number of MNEs already have TCFs in place. Ideally these TCFs cover the worldwide operations of the MNE rather than just the jurisdictions that require a TCF as part of co-operative compliance regimes; where TCFs do already exist this may provide a useful tool to start building trust. Where MNEs adopt TCFs, this may be a useful first step towards co-operative compliance that may encourage tax administrations to adopt the approach. Tax administrations unfamiliar with TCFs may need support in developing processes to test/assess TCFs; such guidance and training could be integrated into capacity building on co-operative compliance.

3.2.4. Business principles

Voluntary business principles on tax are a relatively recent development that provide one way for businesses to clarify what others should expect from their behaviour on tax, and provide an opportunity to introduce some degree of accountability. The questions for the tax administration survey that provided the basis for this report were based on the Business at OECD best practices. While most questions were designed to enable some accountability on performance against the principles, several questions were included to understand the awareness of, and perceived utility of these principles, as well as possible ways to improve them.

An overwhelming majority of officials across regions found that the Business at OECD statement of best practices is useful for improving their relationship with large businesses. However, awareness about these commitments was low. Over 80% of officials in all regions (92% in the LAC region, 87% in Asia, 85% in OECD countries and 80% in Africa) stated that they found the statement of best practices useful, though many had not previously encountered them, with only 23% of officials in Africa, 33% in OECD, 34% in Asia, and 36% in the LAC region stating that they were aware of the best practices prior to taking the survey. In addition, higher levels of awareness of the principles correlate with higher perceptions of usefulness, which suggests that increasing communication on the principles could yield positive results.

In addition to increasing awareness of the principles, there is also scope to improve them. Around 50% of tax officials (48% OECD, 50% LAC, 55% Africa, 60% Asia), stated that the principles could be enhanced, and provided suggestions for improvement.

Some of the suggestions for improvement referred to the number or detail of the commitments. These include developing in greater detail references to transfer pricing and BEPS-related practices (given that the principles were developed prior to the launch of the BEPS Project); clarifying the meaning of some terms (such as "reasonable and relevant"); adding new principles, such as a specific commitment to extend the obligations to all entities in a group ("all related entities, including parent companies, should facilitate the flow of information with other group members"); a principle to avoid the request of deferrals or extensions unless they are duly justified (and never with dilatory purposes); and explicit references to the reparation of environmental damages and externalities, including complying with and supporting environmental taxation legislation, and the commitment to work towards a public-private alliance against corruption. More broadly, participants encouraged entities to commit to disclose relevant information concerning capital gains, transfer prices, new types of transaction or new business processes whenever possible.

Other suggestions indicate areas where there is scope for developing additional guidance. Developing region-specific and country-specific principles adapted to the local context, sector-specific principles to capture sectoral characteristics that might impact compliance, and specific guidance on how large businesses should interact responsibly with the tax authorities in Special Economic Zones (SEZs), were mentioned as important priorities. Administrations proposed developing similar principles for tax officials (which could complement Charters of Taxpayers' Rights) and practical guidance that outlines how officials should behave, and what procedures administrations can put in place, to encourage a positive behaviour from MNEs. Several respondents across regions suggested publishing best practices and case studies that show how the principles translate into practice, including examples of good co-operation with large taxpayers and of good business behaviour, as well as practices for preventing and dealing with audit disputes.

A final set of suggestions focused on the implementation of principles. While some respondents proposed a sanctioning mechanism be developed, others advocated for promoting good behaviour by developing a system of recognition for businesses/MNEs regarded as compliant with the principles. Specific indicators for monitoring the implementation of the commitments (both within administrations and within MNEs) were also mentioned. Regarding awareness-raising, respondents stressed the need to make the statement available in languages other than English (in particular, Spanish and French) and to increase the number of trainings, seminars and communication campaigns to sensitise officials and taxpayers about its existence and importance, including through on-line trainings.

The survey data and roundtable discussions indicated further issues that could be considered for inclusion in a revised statement of best practices. The challenge of obtaining information from overseas was raised in all roundtables as a challenge, and several MNEs suggested that improvements should be possible. Methods for staff recruitment may also be useful to consider; for example MNEs could both commit to supporting training in country, and considering the impact of recruitment on tax administration capacities. In addition, the results may provide suggestions on where further detail concerning best practices may be useful, for example providing more information on what co-operation means in practice and highlighting some of the types of information that may be useful to share (including information that goes beyond strictly tax information, such as value chain descriptions).

Other voluntary principles that have emerged may provide inspiration on how to improve the principles. The B Team which brings together business and other leaders to call for, and demonstrate, a better way of doing business, established a set of responsible tax principles in 2018 (The B Team, 2018[7]), which have been endorsed by 24 MNEs at the time of writing[2]. In addition, The B Team is also publishing a series of case studies on how the principles translate into action within endorsing MNEs[3]. The B Team principles provide more detail on the behaviours expected; as such some of the principles developed by The B Team address issues highlighted in this report. For example, in respect to the relationship with authorities, The B Team principles commit to providing information held in other jurisdictions, where relevant (see (The B Team, 2018[7]) principle 4B), which was identified as a key challenge by many administrations. While The B Team is showing one approach to providing accountability on adherence to voluntary principles, further work is needed. Insofar as the principles map onto TCFs (where these exist), these may provide some degree of accountability, especially where tax administrations are assessing TCFs as part of co-operative compliance programmes. Another option is incorporating principles into the guidelines/expected standards of behaviour for both tax administrations and taxpayers. Providing more examples (as in The B Team case studies) of practical compliance with the principles will be useful in giving administrations the confidence to recognise non-compliance.

One way to increase accountability is for countries to integrate best practices into taxpayers' charters and/or other statements of expectations of behaviour. Given that the best practices have been developed and agreed by MNEs themselves, they represent a ready-made set of standards for tax authorities to use as a reference point. Incorporating best practices into domestic accountability mechanisms could encourage adherence to the best practices, as well as empowering tax administrations to recognise behaviour that falls below the standards expected. Such an approach may also increase awareness of the best practices among subsidiaries of MNEs, especially in developing countries, and among tax administrations.

The primary source for accountability is within the enterprises themselves. Where the principles go beyond legal requirements in a jurisdiction, it is likely to be challenging for tax administrations to hold taxpayers to account. It will therefore be incumbent primarily upon the enterprise to set up systems and processes to ensure compliance with principles. In large multinational organisations, establishing consistent behaviour across all subsidiaries may be challenging, especially where there can be subjectivity in what falls within or outside the organisation's policy. Internal accountability processes may therefore be useful to help ensure consistency throughout the organisation. PricewaterhouseCoopers (PwC) has established Tax Policy Panels (TPP) for this purpose (see Box 3.3)

Box 3.3. PwC Tax Policy Panels

PwC's baseline with respect to tax advice is reflected in a Global Tax Code of Conduct (GTCC). Principles applied are:

1. Tax advice which results in positions taken in a client's tax return must be supported by a credible basis in tax law.

2. No tax advice relies for its effectiveness on any tax authority or having less than the relevant facts. Advice that a PwC firm gives includes consideration of, and is based on, the assumption that the client will make relevant disclosures that both comply with the law and enable tax authorities to make further enquiries should they wish to do so.

3. Tax advice is given in the context of the specific facts and circumstances as provided by the client concerned and is appropriate to those facts and circumstances.

4. Tax advice involves discussion of the wider considerations involved, as appropriate in the circumstances, including economic, commercial and reputational risks and consequences arising from the way stakeholders might view a particular course of action.

---

5. PwC firms advise clients of appropriate options available to them under the law having regard to all of the principles contained in this code.

PwC firms are expected to conduct rigorous technical analysis of advice to clients. But the principles embodied in the GTCC are much broader than just of technical nature. PwC tax advisors are expected to submit projects to Tax Policy Panels (TPP) if certain criteria, including some that are similar to mandatory disclosure hallmarks, are met. A TPP will then review the project against the background of the GTCC and will assess the project beyond its technical merits, in particular consider tax policy, systemic, economic, commercial and reputational risk and the way stakeholders might view a particular course of action. Decisions by TPPs are strong guidance for the practice. Recognising that different PwC firms act in different territories and in different legal cultures, the chairpersons of the TPPs convene regularly in order to discuss matters that have come before the panels; the goal of these meetings is to come to international convergence in review of the cases.

The establishment and operation of PwC's TPPs have contributed to much more holistic tax advice that takes on board the societal context in which tax advice is rendered.

As of 30 June 2021, TPPs had been established in 34 territories. During FY21, over 560 matters were considered and discussed by the TPPs.

Source: PwC

3.2.5. Reducing opportunities for bribery

The survey results indicate a small but worrying perception of bribery in every region. Both taxpayers and tax administrations need to take strong actions to both reduce the opportunity and incentives for bribery.

Clear Codes of Conduct for both tax administrations and MNEs reduce the risk of misconduct. Incorporating examples into these Codes of Conduct (e.g. no gift policy) might help. Insights from behavioural science show that exposing individuals to real-life scenarios of moral dilemmas or conflicts of interest reduces the risk of misbehaviour. When individuals have the opportunity to consider a dilemma beforehand, they are more likely to act with integrity when confronted by it (OECD, 2018[8]). A similar approach could be taken to integrate ethical considerations into technical seminars and training, rather than the usual approach of presenting ethics as a stand-alone issue.

Administrations reported that clear communication protocols in which auditors debrief to colleagues their interactions with the taxpayer has helped in reducing the risk of misbehaviour. Introducing a standard governance process to review large taxpayer audit conclusions, possibly together with statistical analysis of tax collection that could identify inconsistencies, could also be useful. Increasing the number of auditors involved in audits, and as a minimum ensuring no one-to-one meetings between taxpayers and tax administrations, was also cited as a successful policy against misbehaviour.

Governments should ensure that legislative, policy and administrative frameworks support their anti-corruption efforts. The OECD Recommendation on Public Integrity provides a comprehensive framework to foster integrity by combining enforcement and deterrence with the promotion of a culture of integrity. The OECD Public Integrity Handbook (OECD, 2020[9]) provides practical guidance for implementing this Recommendation.

Governments can use legislation to support public integrity in companies. For example, many governments have legislation requiring companies to establish an anti-bribery compliance programme, which includes anti-corruption corporate policies, capacity building, reporting channels, risk management and internal control functions (OECD, 2020[9]).

Governments can combat the supply side of bribery by signing the OECD Convention on Combating Bribery of Foreign Public Officials in International Business Transactions[4]. This anti-corruption instrument criminalises bribery of foreign public officials and reduces incentives by explicitly disallowing the tax deductibility of bribes to foreign public officials. Signatories to the anti-bribery convention commit to establish the bribery of foreign public officials as a domestic offence. Such domestic legislation with extra-territorial reach can be an effective tool to improve business culture. The UK Bribery Act was introduced in 2011 and in section 7 created a 'failure to prevent bribery' offence. Research suggests that this legislation has resulted in a significant change in MNE policy and practices, both within MNEs subject to the Act and their suppliers (see for example (Goldstraw-White and Gill, 2016[10]) and (LeBaron, 2017[11])).

3.3. Transparency and communication

Transparency and communication are closely linked. The roundtable discussions noted that poor communication is likely to affect willingness to be transparent with tax administrations. A number of recommendations were made and best practices identified, not only covering direct communication between taxpayers and administrations but also the wider landscape, including the need to increase the transparency around the processes regulating the relationship between large taxpayers and tax administrations, to build trust among the wider public. Given the findings from the survey that perceptions of co-operativeness are higher than perceptions of trust and openness in the information provided, it seems likely that the challenge in many countries is not participation in the formal processes, but rather improving the commitment to and content of the dialogue.

The roundtables highlighted the willingness of MNEs and tax administrations to facilitate a more open and ongoing dialogue between taxpayers and tax authorities, not only on the occasion of tax audits or assessments, but also on a regular basis. There are various approaches being implemented that increase the available channels of communication between taxpayers and administrations, as well as improving the existing channels. These approaches range from engagement at the time of policy development, to improving requests for information during audits. They have a shared interest in facilitating more effective communication and reduce disputes. While participants in the roundtables were, in general, in favour of enabling greater and more frequent informal dialogue to prevent formal disputes, clear policies and processes are still needed to reduce the risk of creating opportunities for corruption or other improper behaviour.

3.3.1. Multilateral dialogue

Several businesses with experience of the International Compliance Assurance Programme (ICAP) highlighted its benefits in facilitating open and co-operative multilateral engagements between MNEs and tax administrations. While it was acknowledged that ICAP may not be suitable for many developing countries, there was support in the roundtables for providing an avenue for more flexible, higher-level multilateral dialogue between MNE groups and tax administrations.

Providing a route to facilitate multilateral dialogue between MNEs and tax administrations in developing countries outside of ICAP could provide benefits on both sides. As many MNEs have reported challenges with tax administrations understanding their structures and value chains, opportunities to discuss and explain these with several jurisdictions simultaneously could be valuable. For tax administrations, especially those with limited capacities, dialogue with MNEs together with peers could be useful in building skills and understanding. In addition, it would open to MNEs participating to voluntarily provide additional information, such as country by country reports, which may not otherwise be accessible by developing country tax administrations.

Further work is needed to establish the viability of a voluntary multilateral dialogue process, to gauge demand from both MNEs and tax administrations, and, assuming demand exists, to define the parameters of a programme. The OECD will seek to work with others, including Her Majesty's Revenue and Customs capacity development unit, to scope a programme, and if viable to establish pilots.

3.3.2. Stakeholder forums

Several administrations have established forums where stakeholders, including tax officials and MNEs, meet on a regular basis to discuss and offer advice on tax issues and procedures. Tax administrations can use these forums to communicate changes in regulations or processes, or to receive feedback on how bureaucratic procedures can be simplified. Businesses and tax administrations highlighted the benefits of such forums, which can help identify issues that are shared across many taxpayers. In addition, they can also facilitate peer learning, including among taxpayers, and helping improve the capacity to comply.

Some businesses also reported that such forums can improve the perception of the tax administration by demonstrating its willingness to engage positively with taxpayers, as well as its commitment to fairness and transparency with taxpayers. Of course, for such benefits to arise, such forums need to be designed to be open and transparent, with wide participation. It also needs to be shown that such forums have an impact in addressing the issues raised therein.

Consideration should be given to how stakeholders are engaged and when there is a need for forums to focus on specific topics. Where there are common challenges across many taxpayers, broad-based forums can be useful; as issues become more specific, it can be more challenging for forums to play an effective role unless the forums also become more specific. Similarly, relying on joint inputs from taxpayers/taxpayers' associations to such forums can be useful for some issues but can sometimes result in responses that have to generalise to ensure broad agreement across all signatories to the inputs, which can lessen the utility of the inputs to the administration. The Kenya Revenue Authority (KRA) established a Stakeholder Engagement Framework in 2015 to help manage relationships with stakeholders, which provides a range of different modalities to engage with taxpayers and across government. Box 3.4 outlines how stakeholder engagement worked with the introduction of a new Value Added Tax (VAT) refunds formula.

Box 3.4. Stakeholder engagement in Kenya – VAT Refunds Formula

The KRA Stakeholder Engagement Framework was established in 2015, and has been accompanied by a Stakeholder Engagement Secretariat and a mechanism to ensure centralised monitoring and escalation of stakeholder issues.

The introduction of the VAT refund formula as part of the 2017 VAT regulations created challenges, especially for exporters, who were unable to utilise their tax credits and were suffering from cash flow and liquidity challenges.

To address this challenge, the KRA systematically engaged with taxpayers and other stakeholders across government in a series of activities, which ultimately led to the VAT (Amendment) Regulations 2019, implementing a revised formula for refunds, which addresses the challenges taxpayers had been facing. These engagements included:

- Five Weekly Working Groups with technical teams to identify options
- Three monthly Sector/Technical Consultative Forums with industry, to review outputs from working groups

---

- Two Commissioner and Commissioner General Roundtables, held quarterly, enable KRA policy to be determined
- Three consultations with National Treasury – enabled face-to-face dialogue between KRA, Treasury and Industry on policy
- Two parliamentary engagements – to demonstrate the need to review the formula, including evidence from affected stakeholders.

The feedback from this approach has been positive, with the Kenya Association of Manufacturers highlighting both the importance of the revised refund formula and the role of KRA's stakeholder engagement in unlocking challenges the industry had been facing.

Source: Adapted from *Achieving Effective Stakeholder Engagement: A Case Study of VAT Refunds Formula* – available at https://www.kra.go.ke/images/publications/Achieving-Effective-Stakeholder-Engagement_A-Case-Study-of-VAT-Refunds-Formula.pdf

3.3.3. Consultation on new regulations

MNEs and administrations emphasised the benefits of involving taxpayers in the process of drafting new regulations. Bringing taxpayers (and advisors) into the process of designing new regulations can improve the effectiveness of administration as well as strengthening taxpayers' awareness of and confidence in regulations, as they feel a degree of ownership.

Ensuring that consultations are open and transparent is important to build confidence that legitimate consultation is not perceived as (or can morph into) illegitimate lobbying (see Lobbying and public transparency).

3.3.4. Language

Non-Anglophone countries repeatedly highlighted language challenges when dealing with MNEs, as well as when requesting information from other tax administrations. While MNEs may be used to working in English as a common global language, this is not the case in many tax administrations. In many multi-lingual developing countries, especially those with a colonial-era language as an official language, tax administration officials may already be working in a second language. MNEs may also face a challenge in working directly in the local language, as it may prevent senior staff within the MNE from being able to sign off on documents if they are not fluent in the relevant language.

Taxpayers need to respect local language requirements when submitting documents and to provide high-quality translation. Care is particularly needed where there is the risk of specific terminology being interpreted differently, and all parties should seek to ensure a shared understanding of the terms being used. Where language skills are present in the tax administration, administrations may wish to consider accommodating English in certain circumstances, where it may facilitate quicker responses or enhance dialogue with the taxpayers' more senior staff; where translated material is required, sufficient time should be allowed for a high-quality translation. Improving the balance between requesting smaller volumes of information rather than large quantities of data (see Information and data) is likely to make it easier for taxpayers to provide translated information quickly, as will allowing flexibility in terms of format (where feasible).

3.3.5. Information and data

A common theme across the roundtables was the need to focus on securing access to useful information rather than just data. As highlighted in the survey results and the roundtables, tax administrations experience challenges in the responsiveness to requests for information, both from taxpayers, and from other administrations when using exchange of information mechanisms. Meanwhile, businesses raised concerns that requests for information can be unclear, can request information in an unusual form, or can request vast quantities of data rather than specific information. Improving the precision of information requests, versus demanding large quantities of data from taxpayers, provides benefits for both tax administrations and taxpayers. For taxpayers, it reduces the compliance cost/burden, while tax administration is likely to be more efficient if officials do not have to wade through vast quantities of data. It is also likely to help build trust over the longer term as taxpayers become more willing to respond to more limited, comprehensible, requests for information.

Improving the information collected through the initial tax return, as well as ensuring access to data held elsewhere in government and third-party data, can reduce the need for additional information to be requested later. In some cases countries tax returns do not request sufficient information, resulting in a requirement for significant additional data to be requested later. Ensuring the tax return asks for sufficient (but not unnecessary) information is therefore a starting point for improving the information gathering processes. In addition, being able to consult data held elsewhere in government (e.g. customs data) or third-party data, can help the tax administration with risk analysis and reduce and focus further information demands on taxpayers. Access to, and policies and processes for the use of, external data remain a challenge in many developing countries. Removing internal government restrictions on information sharing and gaining access to third-party data may therefore be useful starting points to improve the overall information gathering process, but needs to be accompanied by reforms to enable such data to be used effectively.

A number of recommendations and best practices were identified to improve information gathering by tax administrations. These included:

- **Make use of automated process to both gather and analyse information**. This can reduce compliance costs and ensure that further requests for information are more targeted. Challenges can exist where the tax administration's data interfaces do not align with those of taxpayers, which can make compliance complicated or create confusion with asymmetry of data.

- **Provide opportunities to discuss the objectives of the information request, to determine whether it can be fulfilled more easily.** Examples were given in the roundtables of discussions to identify the specific issues at stake and refining the information requirements accordingly. In some cases, the volume of information requested was just 20% of the initial request. Such discussions have also covered the format in which the data needs to be provided; flexibility on this point can significantly reduce the time taken by taxpayers to comply while still ensuring the information is provided to the tax administration. The earlier such dialogues are opened, the more effective they can be in improving the quality and speed of information requests.

- **Facilitate learning from experience.** Refining the information-gathering exercises in one year only to start from the beginning in subsequent years is both frustrating and inefficient. Continuity of personnel is an obvious means of reducing this risk, especially when as sector-specific knowledge is developed. Other approaches can include post-audit discussions, which enable the administration and taxpayer to review the audit and identify opportunities for compromises/solutions for future years. Such discussions can be minuted (and in some countries provide binding commitments on certain aspects) such that even if personnel changes, there is a record on how to address specific issues.

The timeframes provided for information requests should be considered. Where large volumes of data are requested, especially if in unfamiliar formats, taxpayers can struggle with tight deadlines. Tax administrations should therefore ensure that they are setting realistic deadlines in their requests for information.

The availability of information held in other jurisdictions was cited as a challenge in all roundtables, with tax administrations highlighting challenges with both MNEs and foreign tax administrations responding to requests. While improvements in how and what information is requested from the tax administration is likely to help, this needs to be matched by a willingness from MNEs to provide relevant information held elsewhere when requested, and for foreign tax administrations to be willing to respond to requests for information, including recognising that those requesting information from developing countries that have recently joined exchange of information networks may lack experience in making requests.

Taxpayers require guarantees on information security. Ensuring that their information remains confidential is an important concern of taxpayers, and an important pre-condition before taxpayers are likely to be willing to volunteer any additional information, especially if it is sensitive. As such, tax administrations may need to provide reassurance on (and where necessary improve) information security policies as part of efforts to build trust with taxpayers.

3.3.6. Relationship-building and management

There were various references in the roundtables to the benefits of good interpersonal relationships between taxpayers and tax administrations, as well as recognition of the need to ensure safeguards to prevent such relationships being misused. Consistency of personnel was highlighted as beneficial by many, with both taxpayers and administrations recommending that changes to teams, and especially contact persons, be kept to a minimum. From a behavioural economics perspective, the importance of the messenger effect (i.e. the impact that the perception of the messenger delivering the message has) was highlighted as potentially important for relationships, although it was acknowledged that this has not been explored to any depth in taxpayer/tax administration relationships thus far.

Further research is needed to understand the drivers of effective relationship building between MNEs and tax administrations, especially in developing countries, where there are a range of potential dynamics including power, culture, race, and fluency in English that could influence interpersonal relationships. The OECD will seek to identify partners to investigate these issues further.

The capacity/expertise of staff may be a factor in building effective dialogue between taxpayers and tax administrations. As many developing countries have very small numbers of staff trained in the more complex international tax issues, seeking to engage in a more open dialogue with MNE taxpayers can be challenging. Similarly, where MNEs have small tax functions locally there may not be suitable individuals in country to engage in a more open dialogue. While capacity building can ease these problems over the long term, in the short-term processes will be needed to use the limited resources in an efficient way. This may include looking to clarify which staff will be needed for, and at what stage of, the dialogue between taxpayers and the tax administration.

3.3.7. Governance structures to facilitate dialogue

Clear governance structures and processes for dialogue can reduce confusion among taxpayers and tax administrations. Tax administrations suggested that MNEs could formalise internal governance structures to engage with tax administrations (e.g. Delegation of Authorities, communication policies), thereby facilitating dialogue and co-operation. In addition, ensuring clarity on the role of advisors is important. While advisors can play a mediating role between the tax administration and taxpayers, where the role of advisors is unclear it can increase confusion, for instance where advisors are requested to provide information to which they do not have access from the taxpayer. Clear governance structures in the tax administration are also important. Several businesses in the roundtables raised concerns on lack of clarity of functions and highlighted the importance of clarity on how information they divulged would be used, as well as reassurance that disputes will be dealt with impartially.

Digitisation and automation provide additional tools to govern interactions between taxpayers and administrations. The provision of on-line taxpayer services was perceived by several round-table participants to have resulted in better co-operation from MNEs by facilitating the fulfilment of tax obligations remotely, increasing the speed of payments (and thus fostering respect of deadlines), facilitating payment execution by MNEs for payments requiring authorisation of departments located abroad, and giving the possibility to parent companies to follow tax declarations and payments made by their subsidiaries. In this regard, it was stressed that it is important to test and pilot new on-line services to ensure that they are user-friendly, incorporating feedback from taxpayers while they are being developed.

In some countries, a post-audit dialogue functions as a 'lessons learnt' process between auditor and taxpayer. This allows joint identification of areas for improvement for future audits, thus making future audits easier. In some cases, the process can lead to formal agreements on how certain complex issues will be dealt with in future years.

3.3.8. Lobbying and public transparency

There was relatively little discussion in the roundtables on lobbying, primarily because the participants viewed themselves as less directly involved. Participants perceived lobbying as an activity that takes place elsewhere, often through engagements with politicians and/or more senior officials than were involved in the roundtables. Thus, whereas the perceptions from tax officials on most of the other survey questions were based on their own experience of interactions with taxpayers, in this area the perceptions relate more to what they believe is happening elsewhere.

There was clear agreement that transparency in interactions between taxpayers and officials/politicians can help. Registers of interests, and public records of meetings of ministers and senior officials are used in many countries. Businesses can similarly produce their own publicly available records of meetings.

Clear governance procedures can reduce the potential for illegitimate lobbying. Ensuring that tax incentives have to be provided for in the tax code and cannot be granted arbitrarily by ministers beyond the finance ministry ministers, reduces the scope to lobby for company-specific incentives. Open and transparent consultations and forums for discussing new legislation and regulations build confidence that such laws are not being unduly influenced by lobbying. In respect to individual cases, many of the measures highlighted to assist with reducing bribery are also relevant in respect to lobbying.

Tension in respect to lobbying will remain, as there will always be a perception bias: what one person may perceive as raising a legitimate concern on how a new regulation will affect business, another may perceive as illegitimate lobbying. These perception gaps can be reduced by building trust and providing increased transparency on the policy making process, and contacts between the administration and private sector/lobbyists. The OECD principles for transparency and integrity in lobbying (OECD, 2014[12]) provide useful directions and guidance to help decision makers foster integrity and transparency.

Officials in regions where there is a higher perception of large businesses willing to explain their tax positions and decisions in public appear to have higher trust in the information provided by large businesses, suggesting there may be benefits for MNEs improving public transparency. While this correlation should be treated with caution as the question on how willing large businesses/MNEs are to publicly explain their tax positions was only answered by a fraction of respondents, this may suggest that a willingness to explain taxes in public improves communication and trust in the confidential relationships with tax administrations as well. One challenge for MNEs may be that it is easier to be more open in the HQ country, where senior staff are available to speak to press/parliament as well as the tax administration; further consideration may be needed on how to facilitate a more open dialogue on taxation where subsidiaries operate.

3.4. Capacity-building programmes

As many of the approaches to building trust identified in this report require trained staff to deliver, capacity building programmes play a valuable role, both in tax administrations and in companies/advisory firms. Enhancing capacity in international taxation, especially transfer pricing issues, has consistently been a high priority for capacity-building in tax administrations. The need for capacity-building on international taxation is also recognised by businesses, with lack of expertise in administration of international taxation identified as one of the top ten (out of 21) sources of tax uncertainty for MNEs operating in Africa (6th), Asia (9th) and LAC (10th).

While technical skills are clearly important, there is also a need to build capacity in less tax-specific professional competencies, especially in communication. Such competencies are not often routinely included in existing capacity-building programmes; further work is therefore needed to identify how best to build the full range of skills needed to support the development of effective dialogue between taxpayers and tax authorities.

3.4.1. Tax Inspectors Without Borders

Tax Inspectors Without Borders (TIWB) programmes provide hands-on peer-to-peer support on live cases. This enables the experts providing support to identify specific issues and discuss potential responses with the revenue authority. While much of the focus on TIWB has been on the revenues raised as a direct result of the TIWB engagement in cases (USD 1.6 billion to end 2021), there is also growing anecdotal evidence of the wider impact of TIWB programmes on encouraging compliance.

By working hand-in-hand with tax administrations on live cases, over a sustained period, TIWB programmes provide the opportunity to build capacity not only on technical issues but also on the processes involved in auditing MNEs and the associated professional competencies As outlined in Box 3.5, these programmes are an opportunity to build capacity in several of the areas highlighted in this report, including improving risk analysis and communication. In a growing number of countries where TIWB programmes have run, administrations are reporting impacts beyond revenues from the specific companies audited: compliance from MNEs has been perceived to improve, with increased filing on time and responsiveness.

TIWB is increasingly trying to monitor its impact beyond revenues, recognising that these impacts may have as much, if not more, long-term impact on compliance than additional revenues from individual cases. Figure 3.1 shows the impact of TIWB programmes on auditors' competencies. Tracking impacts beyond revenues is significantly more challenging, and direct causation can be difficult to determine. This is a common challenge in seeking to track capacity building in more abstract areas and creates a risk that focus moves to areas where the impact is easier to track. As the evidence in this report demonstrates, to achieve desired long-term improvements requires a focus on more abstract variables such as trust alongside initiatives to enhance specific technical capacities.

Figure 3.1. Self-reported competencies of auditors participating in TIWB

■ Programme Start   ■ Programme End

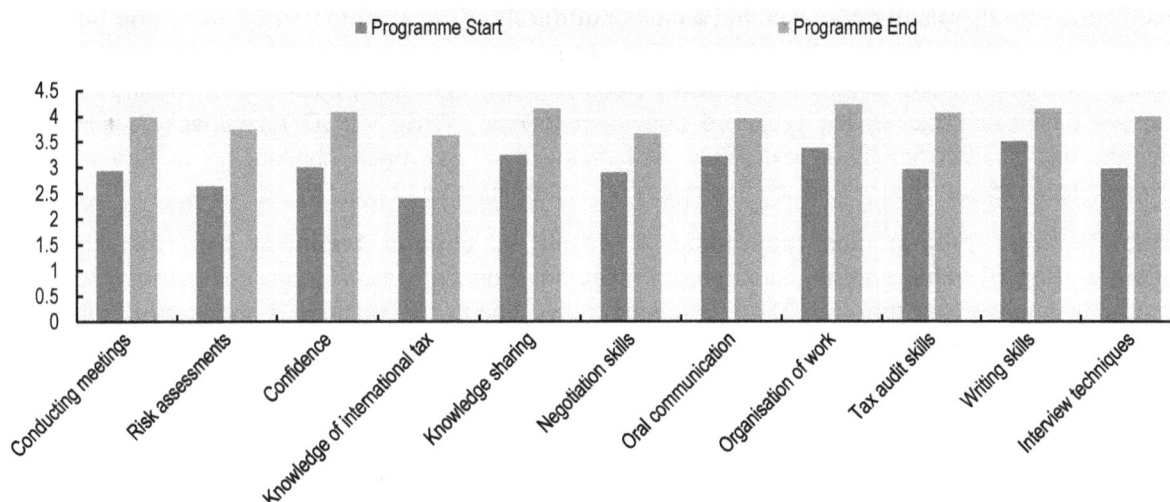

Note: Auditor self-assessments performed at start and end of TIWB programmes in 11 categories, rated on a scale from 1 (Poor) to 5 (Excellent)
Source: TIWB Secretariat

Box 3.5. TIWB's role in improving taxpayer relations

The experience of TIWB programmes shows that efficient administration of the audit process contributes to raising compliance. In a recently completed programme in Côte d'Ivoire's Direction Générale des Impôts (DGI), tax officials conducting audits were faced with generic, absent, incomplete or delayed answers from taxpayers. Some taxpayers even reported in languages that were unknown to the audit team, nullifying the effort and resources deployed by the DGI. Supported by an expert from the Belgium Tax Administration, DGI officials adopted a new audit strategy based on several key factors:

- Standardisation of the audit processes: focusing on strengthening the audit methodology to ensure certainty in the conduct of audits both from the perspective of the tax administration and taxpayers. To that purpose, the DGI invested in an international comparables database to make sure it could challenge taxpayer transactions despite not having domestic arm's length examples. It also created a specialised Transfer Pricing Unit to build up the expertise of its tax officials, further facilitating exchanges with taxpayers' fiscal teams.

- Increased communication with taxpayers: increasing contacts between tax administration and taxpayers requires smooth channels of communications. In this regard, centralising the communication around a key contact fosters taxpayers' ability to follow-up on each request and increase accountability towards the audit process.

- Focus on taxpayer education: helping taxpayers anticipate and adapt to constantly evolving tax legislation, thus raising certainty and trust towards the tax administration and its officials. This may encompass mutual learning opportunities during information sessions or networking events, especially regarding sector-specific situations, which the tax administration may not be aware of.

Overall, facilitating and multiplying the exchanges between taxpayers and managing expectations helps building strong relationships with taxpayers and may lead first to more revenues for the tax administration and in turn to an enhanced tax morale, or voluntary compliance among taxpayers.

Source: TIWB Secretariat

3.4.2. Value chains/business structures

MNEs consistently raised concerns that a lack of understanding around value chains and business structures creates mistrust and confusion. This problem has been apparent for some time, but finding solutions has been challenging. Given that expertise primarily sits within businesses, utilising expertise from the business sector is the preferred option for training. While OECD-led capacity-building with business participation has been extremely well received, it has been challenging to find business representatives to participate. As such, the reach of such training has been limited.

Virtual learning programmes may make it easier to engage business expertise to raise understanding of value chains. Such programmes have become much more common following the restrictions imposed by the COVID-19 pandemic. One option to consider is to develop e-learning programmes in collaboration between the OECD, BIAC and Regional Tax Organisations.

3.4.3. Capacity building within businesses

While most focus on capacity building is on tax administrations, businesses may also need to build their capacities. Such capacity building can enable mutual dialogue to be effective, and reciprocal trust to be built.

Businesses may have particular challenges maintaining standards in more remote jurisdictions, especially where there are limited local staff and infrequent contact with senior management. This problem can be especially marked in jurisdictions where the business has relatively small operations and there is no local tax function, meaning the tax function may be undertaken by the finance staff. In such instances, clear policies/processes are needed to ensure all staff know their responsibilities, and that local staff are effectively supervised by the relevant tax function. It is also important to ensure the dialogue between local and more senior staff is reciprocal, and that senior staff are clear on the differences/challenges that exist in a developing country context to help inform the development of both the local and global approach to tax.

Where businesses have committed to voluntary principles for behaviour on taxation, those principles should be explained to all relevant staff. Some businesses have mandatory staff training on voluntary principles. There may be additional challenges where functions are outsourced to local advisory firms that may have capacity challenges and not be aware of how to interpret a client company's voluntary principles (see Box 3.6 for how Anglo American trains its external suppliers of tax services on its principles). In addition, businesses may need to reflect on how to ensure compliance with their tax principles in different jurisdictions. Jurisdictions with lower capacity and/or less advanced legislation may present greater opportunities for tax planning that were not intended by the authorities; in these cases, tax-planning strategies may require more careful consideration to ensure alignment with principles.

> ### Box 3.6. Anglo American external supplier training
>
> Anglo American is a UK-listed global mining company with headquarters in London whose Tax Strategy[5] and annual Tax & Economic Contribution Reports[6] give information to all stakeholders on how it seeks to meet its ambitions for responsible behaviour in tax.
>
> Anglo American has recognised need to take external advice in relation to its tax affairs, and to work with advisers in partnership to ensure it is compliant with laws and meets all the other elements of its Tax Strategy. However, it has also recognised the risks that could undermine these objectives if those advisers are not clear on the Group's expectations of them, Anglo American has therefore decided to formally educate key suppliers of tax services on key issues for the company.
>
> The training is in the form of a video, introduced by the Group Head of Tax and presented by senior members from across the organisation from Supply Chain, Business Assurance Services as well as the Group Tax Team. It gives practical advice on core components of the Group's core principles and governance in relation to tax. This includes:
>
> - The Group Code of Conduct, which explains (among other things) how decisions are made that are within the spirit of the law, and includes explicit reference to the Tax Strategy and the zero-tolerance approach to tax evasion and facilitation of tax evasion
> - The Group Responsible Sourcing programme, which outlines key requirements and steps for suppliers to demonstrate their ESG and sustainability practices
> - The Group Tax Strategy, including its key principles, pillars, and proof points of how it operates in practice
> - The Group Tax Governance Framework, including Tax Control Frameworks, Group Tax Policies, the Anti-Tax Evasion Strategy, and how compliance with them is monitored
> - The Group's Covid-19 Tax Concessions Policy, which outlines in detail which concessions should never be accepted, and which might be considered where there is a business need (more details are publicly available in the 2020 TEC Report).
> - Expectations of advisers, including understanding and abiding by these policies, knowledge of priorities and red lines, and who to speak to if further guidance is required.
>
> As part of the Tax Control Framework that the Group has implemented, key suppliers globally are required to attest on a yearly basis via an online form they are aware of and in compliance with the policies covered by this training. The training has also been translated into Spanish and Portuguese for the benefit of Anglo American Group Tax's suppliers primarily based in Latin America
>
> Source: Anglo American

References

CIAT (2020), *Manual sobre Gestión de Riesgos de Incumplimiento para Administraciones Tributarias*, https://www.ciat.org/Biblioteca/DocumentosTecnicos/Espanol/2020_Manual-gestion-riesgos_CIAT-SII-FMI.pdf. [5]

Eberhartinger, E. (2021), *Are Risk-based Tax Audit Strategies Rewarded? An Analysis of Corporate Tax Avoidance*, https://doi.org/10.2139/ssrn.3911228. [4]

Goldstraw-White, J. and M. Gill (2016), "Tackling bribery and corruption in the Middle East: perspectives from the front line", *Journal of Financial Crime*, Vol. 23/4, pp. 843-854, https://www.emerald.com/insight/content/doi/10.1108/JFC-08-2015-0040/full/html. [10]

LeBaron, G. (2017), "Steering CSR Through Home State Regulation: A Comparison of the Impact of the UK Bribery Act and Modern Slavery Act on Global Supply Chain Governance", *Global Policy*, Vol. 8/53, pp. 15-28, https://doi.org/10.1111/1758-5899.12398. [11]

Martini, M. (2022), "A review of Brazil approaches to cooperative compliance in light of International Tax Practice and the OECD concept", *Intertax*, Vol. 50/2, pp. 177-195, https://kluwerlawonline.com/journalarticle/Intertax/50.2/TAXI2022016. [2]

OECD (2020), *OECD Public Integrity Handbook*, OECD Publishing, Paris, https://doi.org/10.1787/ac8ed8e8-en. [9]

OECD (2018), *Behavioural Insights for Public Integrity: Harnessing the Human Factor to Counter Corruption*, OECD Public Governance Reviews, OECD Publishing, Paris, https://doi.org/10.1787/9789264297067-en. [8]

OECD (2016), *Co-operative Tax Compliance: Building Better Tax Control Frameworks*, OECD Publishing, Paris, https://doi.org/10.1787/9789264253384-en. [1]

OECD (2014), *Lobbyists, Governments and Public Trust, Volume 3: Implementing the OECD Principles for Transparency and Integrity in Lobbying*, OECD Publishing, https://doi.org/10.1787/9789264214224-en. [12]

OECD (2011), *OECD Guidelines for Multinational Enterprises, 2011 Edition*, OECD Publishing, Paris, https://doi.org/10.1787/9789264115415-en. [6]

Owens, J. (ed.) (2021), *Cooperative Compliance: A Multi-Stakeholder And Sustainable Approach To Taxation*, Wolters Kluwer, https://law-store.wolterskluwer.com/s/product/cooperative-compliance/01t4R00000OVRsq. [3]

The B Team (2018), *A New Bar for Responsible Tax: The B Team Responsible Tax Principles*, https://bteam.org/assets/reports/A-New-Bar-for-Responsible-Tax.pdf. [7]

Notes

1 International Survey on Revenue Administration – this is a collaboration between CIAT, IMF, IOTA and OECD which collectively surveys 156 tax administrations.

2 https://bteam.org/our-thinking/news/responsible-tax

3 https://bteam.org/our-thinking/news/the-b-team-responsible-tax-principles-in-action-shells-dedication-to-building-trust-among-all-stakeholders

4 https://www.oecd.org/corruption/oecdantibriberyconvention.htm

[5]https://www.angloamerican.com/~/media/Files/A/Anglo American-Group/PLC/investors/annual-reporting/2021/tax-strategy-december-2021.Pdf

[6]https://www.angloamerican.com/~/media/Files/A/Anglo American-Group/PLC/investors/annual-reporting/2022/tax-and-economic-contribution-report-2021.pdf

4 Summary and key recommendations

This chapter provides a summary of key findings of the research, and some key recommendations for all stakeholders to consider in their efforts to improve tax morale.

Surveys of both tax administration officials and MNEs, combined with discussion in roundtables, suggests there is significant scope to improve tax morale of MNEs, and highlights the importance of building trust. While the surveys used in this report show perceptions, and are therefore subject to caveats, they suggest that while some MNEs demonstrate high tax morale, through adherence to their voluntary best practices, there is still work to do, especially in those regions where the majority of MNEs appear to be failing to demonstrate their adherence to some best practices. Building trust it vital, but is a multi-faceted challenge, with transparency and communication as key issues to address. While it is naïve to expect there to be high tax morale in all MNEs and permanently good relationships with the tax administration, there is clearly scope for improvement, as well as good practice to build from, in all regions.

Improving relationships is a win-win outcome for taxpayers and tax administrations. MNEs have repeatedly highlighted the importance they attach to tax certainty and reducing disputes, while tax administrations have much to gain through being able to better prioritise their enforcement activities on high-risk taxpayers.

Responsibility for building trust and improving transparency and communication is shared between taxpayers (and advisors) and administrations. Building trust and improving communication requires actions by both sides in any relationship, and this is no different in tax. This was recognised by participants in the roundtable discussions that informed this report, demonstrating that there is willingness from all sides to identify changes and improvements that they can make. There are a range of actions and good practices identified during the roundtables and outlined in this report that may help. These cover compliance and audit strategies, improving expectations and accountability of behaviour, transparency and communication, as well as capacity-building.

There is strong interest in moving towards a co-operative compliance approach. This is likely to be a long journey for many developing countries but there are many steps along the way that will help build trust. The move towards co-operative compliance is global, and a growing number of developing countries are adopting, at least, elements of, the approach. Co-operative compliance cannot be implemented quickly. It requires a certain degree of mutual trust as a pre-condition, as well as clear regulations and processes to govern the system. As such, especially where trust is currently lowest, a range of other actions to build the foundations for the introduction of co-operative compliance will be needed first. Some of these steps may by relatively simple to introduce, for example improved communication, and could be effective in creating a positive dynamic between taxpayers and tax administrations.

Improving expectations of, and accountability for, behaviour will be key for building trust. The survey data from both tax administrations and MNEs highlight that expectations, and predictability, of behaviour is a challenge, especially in developing countries. Changing perceptions here may be hard, as perceptions can remain even as behaviour has begun to change, preventing the emergence of a virtuous cycle of increased expectations. It is for this reason that accountability is also needed, to help demonstrate the commitment to standards of behaviour, and to provide reassurance that (where there is a genuine commitment to change) when expectations are not met there is a process to address the issues and avoid the undermining of trust that has been built.

Voluntary business principles are widely recognised as useful but their full potential has not yet been realised. The survey results show that businesses have not yet been able to demonstrate widespread adherence to the most widely endorsed voluntary standards more than eight years after they were agreed. While there is broad agreement that such principles can play a role in building trusted relationships with tax administrations, there clearly remains work to do to demonstrate their implementation in practice and improve accountability. In recognition of this, Business at OECD has committed to reviewing their statement of best practices in light of the findings of the survey and roundtable discussions.

Increasing informal dialogue between taxpayers and administrations will need to be accompanied by effective transparency to maintain trust from other stakeholders. There was strong support in the roundtable discussions for actions to facilitate improved communication between taxpayers and administrations, especially less formal dialogue, that can help focus formal dialogue on the key issues and/or resolve issues before they become formal disputes. While such approaches appear desirable, they also increase the risk of illegitimate behaviour (including corruption/bribery); as such, clear safeguards and effective transparency are needed to reassure stakeholders that they can have trust in the systems being used. Without such safeguards, there is a risk that the tax morale of other taxpayers (e.g. SMEs and individuals) may be undermined if they perceive the dialogue between the tax administration and MNEs as illegitimate (e.g. granting 'deals').

Capacity-building initiatives, in both the private and public sector, can address some of the barriers to building trust but new approaches may be needed. There is growing evidence of the potential of capacity-building initiatives such as TIWB to improve the relationships between tax administrations and MNEs. The impact on compliance, rather than enforcement, is an increasing focus for monitoring impacts. While the technical skills that are usually the focus of technical assistance are vital, there is also a need to build capacities in broader professional competencies such as effective communication, negotiation and dialogue with taxpayers, which has been less of a focus of technical assistance thus far. Businesses also need to reflect on their own capacity-building needs, especially in developing country operations, to ensure that their staff are aware of, and able to meet, the expectations of both their own businesses principles and tax administrations.

While some of the best practices identified in this report are immediately actionable, further work is needed. This report provides some best practices from both countries and businesses that can be implemented immediately, where appropriate, and in some cases (e.g. TCFs) where some guidance already exists. It also outlines new ideas that require further scoping. This report also identifies some areas where capacity building may need to be further developed, such as on value chains and co-operative compliance, or where further research is needed, such as better understanding how cultural differences and perception biases may affect trust in tax. As such, there is a range of actions that could be taken in response to the findings in this report, these include:

- **Encourage the development of country-level strategies to build trust and tax morale.** Especially where current levels of trust are low and relationships strained, (re)building trust will take time and require a sustained effort. Developing a clear strategy, in consultation between tax administrations, MNEs and other relevant stakeholders, can build momentum for the changes identified, as well as support not only from the government and MNEs, but also from development partners to assist in implementation. Such strategies may incorporate, where relevant, approaches outlined in this report; further collation and dissemination of best practices and guidance may help countries as they develop such strategies.

- **Enhance existing capacity building, and where necessary develop new capacity building tools, guidance and programmes to respond to the demands identified in this report and roundtables.** There is clear potential for further/new capacity building in several areas:

  o Co-operative compliance – building on the existing publications on co-operative compliance, further guidance and training could be developed, with a particular emphasis on how to build co-operative compliance in developing countries.

  o Value chains – new guidance and training could be developed on value chains in different sectors. Given the challenges that have previously been faced in obtaining private sector participation in such training, it may be beneficial to focus on e-learning courses initially, which will allow more flexible engagement from those contributing.

  o Professional skills and ethics – existing capacity-building programmes may often cover aspects of professional skills and ethics, but there is scope to pay more attention to these issues and ensure that they are more systematically addressed and prioritised.

- **(Re)invigorate the role of business principles/best practices.** The survey responses highlighted both support for business principles/best practices and the unfulfilled potential of them.

There is scope for business to look both at the principles/best practices themselves, and how they can be improved, as well as how businesses hold themselves accountable to such principles. There is also scope for tax administrations (and other stakeholders) to identify ways to hold businesses to these standards, for example in integrating them into domestic accountability frameworks.

- **Explore the feasibility of voluntary multilateral dialogue**. While the roundtable participants showed an interest in creating opportunities for voluntary multilateral dialogue between MNEs and multiple tax administrations, the demand and practical feasibility has not been explored more widely. A feasibility study would therefore be useful, and if positive could be followed by a pilot programme.

- **Undertake further research on what influences effective relationship building.** Building trust and effective relationships is clearly a key issue identified in this report. To a large degree, the actions that need to be taken will be context specific. There may, however, be value in further research to increase understanding of the role of factors such as perception bias in influencing relationships between taxpayers and tax administrations.

- **Support an increased commitment by all stakeholders to building trust and tax morale.** As highlighted in this report, actions are needed by all stakeholders to build the trust that tax morale relies upon. Delivering such actions will require commitments of resources but also an approach that encourages openness, transparency, and dialogue. For some (possibly many) taxpayers and tax administrations, such an approach may be somewhat alien and will need sustained encouragement from all stakeholders.

As part of the OECD's tax morale workstream, the OECD will look to identify and work with a range of partners to pursue the actions identified in this report, including integrating them into the OECD's tax and development capacity-building efforts where possible. The OECD will also seek to identify opportunities to enhance the broader dialogue on tax morale, going beyond the specific focus on the role of trust in this report. Where possible, the OECD will seek to make links and work with other stakeholders, who may have different tools to influence tax morale, for example with investors who are increasingly focusing on tax, especially with respect to ESG considerations.

Annex A. Tax administration officials perceptions survey results

Table A A.1. Perceptions of large business/MNE behaviour

1. When thinking about the large/MNE business in your country, are the following statements accurate?:				
	Africa	Asia	OECD	LAC
A. Large/MNE business are open and transparent with the revenue authorities with their tax affairs, and relevant information				
Yes, almost all large/MNE businesses	6%	9%	13%	4%
Yes, most large/MNE businesses	38%	45%	51%	27%
About half of large/MNE businesses	19%	21%	22%	26%
No, only some large/MNE businesses	30%	21%	12%	33%
Almost no large/MNE businesses	7%	4%	1%	10%
B. The tax information provided by large MNEs to the tax authorities can be trusted.				
Yes, almost all large/MNE businesses	4%	8%	15%	3%
Yes, most large/MNE businesses	39%	45%	59%	34%
About half of large/MNE businesses	24%	28%	21%	25%
No, only some large/MNE businesses	26%	17%	5%	31%
Almost no large/MNE businesses	7%	2%	1%	7%
C. Large businesses/MNEs respond to information requests from the tax authority within the time limits specified.				
Yes, almost all large/MNE businesses	16%	17%	27%	11%
Yes, most large/MNE businesses	34%	45%	48%	44%
About half of large/MNE businesses	18%	22%	19%	22%
No, only some large/MNE businesses	27%	13%	5%	16%
Almost no large/MNE businesses	5%	2%	1%	7%
D. Large/MNE business hand the relevant information requested in the correct form.				
Yes, almost all large/MNE businesses	9%	14%	24%	5%
Yes, most large/MNE businesses	45%	47%	51%	39%
About half of large/MNE businesses	21%	22%	20%	25%
No, only some large/MNE businesses	19%	15%	4%	21%
Almost no large/MNE businesses	6%	2%	1%	9%
E. Large/MNE business are willing to cooperate with the tax authorities.				
Yes, almost all large/MNE businesses	13%	17%	24%	8%
Yes, most large/MNE businesses	48%	51%	60%	41%
About half of large/MNE businesses	20%	19%	10%	23%
No, only some large/MNE businesses	18%	13%	4%	21%
Almost no large/MNE businesses	2%	1%	2%	7%

2. When thinking about large/MNE businesses in your country, please rate the following statements as per the scale

	Africa	Asia	OECD	LAC

A. *Against the request of tax authorities, large/MNE business answer the tax authorities in an open transparent and straightforward manner.*

	Africa	Asia	OECD	LAC
Almost all large/MNE businesses	4%	8%	13%	4%
Most large/MNE businesses	39%	39%	51%	34%
About half of large/MNE businesses	17%	29%	30%	27%
Some large/MNE businesses	36%	21%	5%	28%
Almost no large/MNE businesses	4%	3%	1%	8%

B. *Large/MNE business pay their tax liabilities within the established due date (or within a reasonable time-frame where no such due dates are established).*

	Africa	Asia	OECD	LAC
Almost all large/MNE businesses	22%	23%	50%	34%
Most large/MNE businesses	58%	54%	42%	51%
About half of large/MNE businesses	11%	13%	6%	9%
Some large/MNE businesses	8%	9%	2%	5%
Almost no large/MNE businesses	2%	2%	1%	1%

3. When information requested by the tax authorities was not available from the taxpayer, the MNE/large business involved provided a justified explanation and collaborated with the authorities?

	Africa	Asia	OECD	LAC
Almost always provided	8%	8%	21%	12%
In most cases	42%	45%	57%	38%
In some cases	40%	38%	18%	40%
In most cases did not	9%	7%	1%	8%
Almost never	1%	1%	2%	2%

4. In case of a misunderstanding of the law from tax authorities, are business usually cooperative to identify the issue and attempt to resolve it?

	Africa	Asia	OECD	LAC
Almost all large/MNE businesses.	15%	18%	17%	11%
Most large/MNE businesses.	48%	50%	61%	38%
About half of large/MNE businesses.	9%	15%	16%	18%
Some large/MNE businesses.	27%	15%	5%	21%
Almost no large/MNE businesses.	1%	1%	2%	12%

5. In your Tax Administration, when auditing a large/MNE business, how often do significant disputes arise?

	Africa	Asia	LAC	OECD
Almost always.	14%	8%	27%	4%
Very often.	35%	35%	41%	29%
In some cases.	46%	48%	27%	59%
Very rarely.	6%	7%	6%	9%
Never.	0%	1%	0%	0%

6. To what extent do you agree with the following statement? Answer according to the following scale:				
"When a disagreement has been found between a large/MNE business and the tax authorities, the business involved has been open to consider dispute resolution procedures (mediation/ arbitration)."				
	Africa	Asia	OECD	LAC
Almost all large/MNE businesses are open to resolution procedures.	17%	18%	14%	9%
Most large/MNE businesses are open to resolution procedures.	44%	39%	43%	28%
About half of large/MNE businesses are open to resolution procedures.	11%	14%	17%	14%
Some large/MNE businesses are open to resolution procedures.	25%	25%	20%	25%
Almost no large/MNE businesses are open to resolution procedures.	4%	4%	6%	24%

7. In your experience, when discussing/seeking to resolve disputed issues with large/MNE business, the attitude of MNEs/Large businesses has been:				
	Africa	Asia	OECD	LAC
Cooperative, in almost all cases.	24%	23%	35%	17%
Cooperative, in some cases.	66%	56%	46%	51%
Neither cooperative nor non-cooperative.	5%	12%	14%	15%
Non-cooperative, in some cases.	5%	8%	5%	13%
Not cooperative at all.	1%	1%	0%	5%

8. In the course of negotiations or alternative dispute resolution procedures, large/MNE business have acted in good faith and have not tried to exert illegal influence in the process:				
	Africa	Asia	OECD	LAC
Almost always acted in good faith.	9%	14%	31%	11%
In most cases acted in good faith.	45%	47%	45%	36%
In some cases acted in good faith.	41%	28%	15%	35%
Never acted in good faith.	1%	2%	0%	6%
My jurisdiction doesn't contemplate alternative dispute resolution procedures.	4%	8%	10%	13%

9. In terms of their tax behaviour, do you think that local businesses, in comparison to MNEs...:				
	Africa	Asia	OECD	LAC
Local businesses are more compliant than MNEs.	19%	15%	21%	24%
Local businesses are equally compliant as MNEs.	51%	51%	40%	45%
Local businesses are less compliant than MNEs.	30%	35%	39%	31%

10. To what extent does your country provide tax incentives to large/MNE business (in general legislation, not bilateral contracts) as a tool to attract investments?				
	Africa	Asia	OECD	LAC
To a large extent (i.e. almost all large/MNE businesses are eligible).	24%	22%	15%	26%
To some extent.	35%	33%	34%	18%
Only for particular sectors.	38%	35%	10%	47%
To a small extent.	1%	4%	14%	6%
We do not offer tax incentives to large/MNE business.	2%	6%	27%	3%

11. Do you think that most large/MNE businesses utilise tax incentives in the way your home government/your legislation intended? Answer in terms of ratio of all firms:

	Africa	Asia	OECD	LAC
Almost all large/MNE businesses use tax incentives as intended.	10%	20%	18%	13%
Most large/MNE businesses use tax incentives as intended.	40%	38%	52%	35%
About half of large/MNE businesses use tax incentives as intended.	11%	25%	15%	16%
Some large/MNE businesses use tax incentives as intended.	33%	12%	12%	29%
Almost no large/MNE businesses use tax incentives as intended.	5%	4%	2%	7%

12. When thinking about the large/MNE business in your country, are the following statements accurate?:

	Africa	Asia	OECD	LAC
A. *"Businesses lobby the government to obtain individual tax incentives outside of the existing legislation."*				
Almost all large/MNE businesses	12%	5%	8%	17%
Most large/MNE businesses	19%	16%	16%	30%
About half of large/MNE businesses	7%	14%	14%	10%
Only some large/MNE businesses	42%	44%	37%	31%
Almost no large/MNE businesses	20%	21%	25%	12%
B. "Businesses seek to claim tax incentives/exemptions that are not in the statutory, regulatory or administrative framework."				
Almost all large/MNE businesses	8%	4%	5%	12%
Most large/MNE businesses	15%	16%	7%	21%
About half of large/MNE businesses	9%	12%	11%	10%
Only some large/MNE businesses	39%	39%	41%	34%
Almost no large/MNE businesses	29%	28%	35%	22%

13. Does your tax administration have clear guidelines/guidance/procedures to manage the relationship between the revenue authorities and large/MNE business?

	Africa	Asia	OECD	LAC
Yes, there is a detailed procedure in place.	52%	53%	50%	35%
To some extent: there is a limited/general procedure in place.	36%	38%	37%	47%
No, there is no specific procedure in place.	11%	9%	13%	18%

14. Is it your impression that most Large/MNE businesses follow these guidelines/ procedures when dealing with tax authority officials?:

	Africa	Asia	OECD	LAC
Yes, almost all large/MNE businesses.	18%	20%	27%	13%
Yes, most large/MNE businesses.	60%	56%	51%	45%
About half of large/MNE businesses.	9%	13%	11%	14%
No, only some large/MNE businesses.	7%	6%	6%	19%
No, almost no large/MNE businesses.	6%	5%	5%	10%

15. Large/MNE business usually do not attempt to bribe tax officials in order to obtain beneficial outcomes. Answer, degree of agreeing:

	Africa	Asia	OECD	LAC
Almost no large/MNE businesses attempt to bribe tax officials.	29%	51%	81%	41%
Some large/MNE businesses attempt to bribe tax officials.	50%	26%	5%	31%
About half of large/MNE businesses attempt to bribe tax officials.	5%	7%	4%	8%
Almost all large/MNE businesses attempt to bribe tax officials.	9%	10%	7%	12%
Most large/MNE businesses attempt to bribe tax officials.	7%	5%	3%	8%

16. In my experience, in my country, when asked to explain their tax practices publicly (i.e. to the media, civil society, parliament) the approach of large businesses/MNEs has been:

	Africa	Asia	OECD	LAC
Willing to explain their position, in most cases.	19%	29%	41%	13%
Refused to publicly discuss their taxation practices, in most cases.	20%	15%	21%	19%
I have never encountered this case.	61%	56%	38%	68%

17. Had you heard about the Business at OECD Statement on Best Practices for Engaging with Tax Authorities in Developing Countries before taking this survey?

	Africa	Asia	OECD	LAC
Yes.	23%	34%	33%	36%
No.	77%	66%	67%	64%

18. Do you find the Business at OECD Statement on Best Practices useful in improving the relationship between businesses and the tax authorities?

	Africa	Asia	OECD	LAC
Yes.	80%	87%	85%	92%
No.	20%	13%	15%	8%

19. Do you think that the Business at OECD Statement on Best Practices could be improved?

	Africa	Asia	OECD	LAC
Yes.	55%	60%	48%	50%
No.	45%	40%	52%	50%

Note: Simple regional average. Countries are weighted so that no country represents more than 10% of their regional sample
Source: OECD (2020) Survey on MNEs and Big Four Firms tax behaviour

Table A A.2. Perceptions of Big Four behaviour

20. To what extent do you agree with the following statements based on principles set out by the Big Four?
"Big Four firms in my jurisdiction...."

	Africa	Asia	OECD	LAC
A. *Are cooperative with the tax authorities.*				
Yes, in the majority of the cases.	50%	45%	58%	27%
Yes, in some cases.	38%	44%	34%	41%
Only in few cases.	11%	7%	8%	26%
Never.	2%	4%	0%	6%
B. *Only promote tax planning aligned with substance (i.e. Do not promote artificial tax planning structures).*				
Yes, in the majority of the cases.	19%	22%	29%	17%
Yes, in some cases.	49%	53%	45%	44%
Only in few cases.	28%	21%	23%	30%
Never.	5%	5%	3%	9%
C. *Follow the spirit/intention of tax laws (i.e. do not try to exploit loopholes in national legislation to obtain tax advantages for their clients).*				
Yes, in the majority of the cases.	23%	26%	22%	19%
Yes, in some cases.	37%	45%	48%	36%
Only in few cases.	33%	24%	24%	33%
Never.	7%	5%	6%	12%
D. *Are transparent with the tax authorities, providing all relevant information when requested.*				
Yes, in the majority of the cases.	26%	27%	31%	18%
Yes, in some cases.	46%	46%	52%	45%
Only in few cases.	24%	22%	15%	30%
Never.	4%	6%	2%	6%

21. In my opinion there is a role for the Big 4 to be contracted to provide services to the government in (tick all that apply):

	Africa	Asia	OECD	LAC
Advising on domestic tax policy.	52%	45%	25%	22%
Advising on international tax policy.	55%	49%	31%	30%
Advising on how to improve tax administration	55%	43%	31%	25%
Providing technical training to tax officials.	38%	38%	32%	33%
Outsourcing of tax collection functions.	17%	7%	2%	7%

22. In your opinion, do the activities and advice of the Big 4 encourage their clients to:

	Africa	Asia	OECD	LAC
Be more compliant and willing to pay tax in my country.	60%	65%	40%	33%
Have no impact on their clients' compliance and willingness to pay tax.	26%	24%	34%	31%
Be less compliant and less willing to pay tax in my country.	14%	11%	26%	36%

23. In comparison to local tax advisers, do you think that the Big 4 firms:

	Africa	Asia	OECD	LAC
Advise their clients to be more aggressive in their tax strategies.	45%	43%	41%	58%
Advise their clients to be less aggressive in their tax strategies.	20%	23%	16%	12%
There is no difference in the way local advisers and the Big Four firms advise their clients.	35%	34%	43%	30%

24. In your opinion, to what degree do the Big 4 firms seek to use their power to lobby/influence in favour of their clients?:

	Africa	Asia	OECD	LAC
A. *To influence decisions of the tax authority on individual cases.*				
They don't have the power to lobby/influence.	22%	23%	18%	26%
Their power to lobby/influence is used legitimately.	40%	47%	57%	33%
They sometimes use their power illegitimately.	35%	26%	19%	29%
They often use their power illegitimately.	4%	4%	6%	12%
B. *To influence the tax policies and laws of the country.*				
They don't have the power to lobby/influence.	23%	21%	11%	25%
Their power to lobby/influence is used legitimately.	43%	53%	62%	38%
They sometimes use their power illegitimately.	27%	20%	22%	22%
They often use their power illegitimately.	7%	6%	6%	15%

Note: Simple regional average. Countries are weighted so that no country represents more than 10% of their regional sample
Source: OECD (2020) Survey on MNEs and Big Four Firms tax behaviour

Table A A.3. Perceptions on staff retention

26. Finally, the OECD is also interested in understanding better the challenges of staff retention. In the past 5 years in your team, what percentage of staff has been lost to the private sector?

	Africa	Asia	OECD	LAC
0% of our staff has gone to the private sector in the last 5 years	34%	37%	17%	27%
10-20% of our staff.	50%	47%	58%	51%
21-40% of our staff.	10%	10%	21%	13%
41-60% of our staff.	3%	5%	3%	8%
More than 60% of our staff.	2%	1%	1%	1%

27. And to the Big Four firms?	Africa	Asia	OECD	LAC
0% of our staff has gone to the private sector in the last 5 years	52%	54%	31%	55%
10-20% of our staff.	38%	36%	59%	37%
21-40% of our staff.	8%	7%	10%	6%
41-60% of our staff.	2%	2%	0%	1%
More than 60% of our staff.	1%	1%	1%	1%

28. In the past 5 years in your team, how often has your Administration recruited staff from the private sector and/or Big Four firms?	Africa	Asia	OECD	LAC
0% of our staff has gone to the private sector in the last 5 years	55%	54%	37%	34%
10-20% of our staff.	30%	35%	47%	40%
21-40% of our staff.	9%	7%	13%	15%
41-60% of our staff.	4%	2%	3%	7%
More than 60% of our staff.	2%	2%	1%	5%

29. In your opinion, what are the main reasons why MNEs and/or the Big Four seek to hire public officials working on tax? (tick all that apply):	Africa	Asia	OECD	LAC
To access their experience in working within the tax administration.	81%	57%	70%	76%
To gain access to the networks and contacts of public officials.	42%	38%	39%	34%
Because they are better trained or more qualified than staff in the private sector.	34%	28%	39%	22%
To directly influence an ongoing tax dispute.	28%	15%	12%	19%
Other	12%	2%	1%	3%

Note: Simple regional average. Countries are weighted so that no country represents more than 10% of their regional sample
Source: OECD (2020) Survey on MNEs and Big Four Firms tax behaviour

Annex B. MNE Tax Certainty Survey Results

Table A B.1. Regional breakdown of responses from MNEs to question on the sources of tax uncertainty

		Africa		Asia		LAC		OECD	
		Mean	Rank	Mean	Rank	Mean	Rank	Mean	Rank
Legal systems	Unclear, poorly drafted tax legislation	3.7	1	3.4	8	3.6	8	3.3	2
	Complexity in the tax legislation	3.2	16	3.2	12	3.7	3	3.2	3
	Frequent changes in the statutory tax system, regulations and guidance	3.1	19	3.0	20	3.5	15	3.2	4
	Retroactive changes to tax law	3.1	18	3.1	16	3.2	19	2.9	11
	Lack of statute of limitations	2.8	21	2.8	21	2.8	21	2.4	19
	Uncertainty about the ability to obtain withholding tax relief	3.7	2	3.4	6	3.5	13	2.7	16
Tax administration	Considerable bureaucracy to comply with tax legislation	3.6	4	3.6	2	3.9	1	3.3	1
	Unpredictable or inconsistent treatment by the tax authority	3.7	3	3.9	1	3.9	2	3.1	6
	Incentive structure of tax administration not aligned with a fair treatment of taxpayers	3.3	15	3.1	17	3.4	16	2.7	15
	General poor relationship with the tax authority	3.0	20	3.0	19	3.1	20	2.7	17
	Inability to achieve early certainty pro-actively through rulings or other similar mechanisms	3.4	9	3.4	4	3.5	11	2.9	9
	Corruption in the tax system	3.3	14	3.2	13	3.7	6	2.4	20
Dispute resolutions	Lengthy decision making of the courts, tribunals or other relevant bodies	3.4	8	3.3	10	3.7	4	3.1	5
	Unpredictable and inconsistent treatment by the courts	3.3	11	3.4	5	3.6	7	2.9	12
	Lack of published decisions clarifying interpretation	3.3	13	3.2	14	3.2	18	2.6	18
	Corruption in the adjudication system	3.3	12	3.1	18	3.5	12	2.3	21
International dimensions	Inconsistencies between tax authorities on their interpretations of international tax standards	3.6	5	3.6	3	3.7	5	3.1	7
	Conflicts between international standards	3.1	17	3.4	7	3.4	17	2.8	14
	Tax legislation not in line with the evolution of new business models	3.4	10	3.2	15	3.6	9	3.1	8
	Lack of understanding of international business	3.5	7	3.3	11	3.5	14	2.9	10
	Lack of expertise in tax administration on aspects of international taxation	3.5	6	3.3	9	3.5	10	2.9	13

Note: Results for the question, 'Please identify in your experience how important each of the below factors has been in increasing the overall uncertainty on tax issues in the countries you have selected?' The respondents could choose from a scale from 5 to 1, where 5 is extremely important and lower number Indicate the factor is progressively less important. Not all respondents scored each factor, the number of responses per factor is recorded in the Obs column. The Rank column indicates the ranking (1-25) of each factor for each region.
The question represented in this table was asked separately for each country selected by the respondents, each respondent could select a maximum of 4 countries.
Source: OECD (2016) Tax certainty survey

Table A B.2. Regional breakdown of responses to question on which tools/approaches are most important to improving tax certainty

		Africa		Asia		LAC		OECD	
		Mean	**Rank**	**Mean**	**Rank**	**Mean**	**Rank**	**Mean**	**Rank**
Tax Policy Design and Legislation	Changes in statutory tax system announced in advance	4.1	6	3.9	6	4.0	4	3.9	6
	Detailed guidance in tax regulations	4.3	1	4.0	3	4.0	6	4.0	4
	Reduced length and complexity of the tax legislation	3.8	9	3.6	13	3.9	8	3.8	8
	Reduced frequency of changes in the tax legislation	4.1	3	3.8	7	3.9	9	4.1	1
	Timely consultation with taxpayers when changes are introduced	4.0	7	3.6	12	3.9	11	3.7	10
	Domestic tax legislation in line with international taxation standards	4.1	5	4.1	2	4.1	2	3.9	5
	Reduction of bureaucracy to comply with tax legislation	4.1	4	3.7	9	4.1	3	4.0	2
	International consensus on general principles for tax certainty	3.7	12	3.9	5	3.7	13	3.7	13
	Streamlined and effective withholding tax relief reclaim systems	3.5	18	3.7	8	3.6	17	3.6	16
	The use of bright line rules	3.6	16	3.4	17	3.5	19	3.4	18
Tax Administration	Increased transparency from tax administrations in relation to their compliance approaches	3.7	13	3.7	10	4.0	5	3.8	7
	Increased transparency from tax administrations in relation to their risk assessment protocols	3.6	17	3.5	14	3.8	12	3.7	11
	Co-operative compliance programmes in a single jurisdiction	3.5	19	3.2	21	3.5	20	3.4	20
	The existence of simplified approaches for tax compliance e g safe harbours	3.9	8	3.5	16	3.7	14	3.5	17
	Advance pricing arrangement APA in a single jurisdiction	3.5	20	3.4	19	3.5	21	3.3	21
	Other rulings regimes	3.4	23	3.1	22	3.4	24	3.1	24
	Timely communication of tax authority during tax audits	3.7	14	3.4	18	3.6	15	3.6	14
	Capacity Building Programmes for tax authorities	3.4	22	3.0	24	3.4	22	3.1	23
	Efficient communication between taxpayers and administration e g by digital means	3.8	10	3.3	20	3.9	10	3.7	12
Dispute Resolution	Effective domestic dispute resolution regimes	4.3	2	4.1	1	4.2	1	4.0	3
	Mutual agreement procedure MAP	3.7	15	3.9	4	4.0	7	3.8	9
	Mandatory Binding Arbitration	3.8	11	3.6	11	3.6	18	3.6	15
Specific International Dimensions	Multilateral co-operative compliance programmes in collaboration with other jurisdictions	3.3	24	3.0	23	3.4	23	3.3	22
	Multilateral APAs in collaboration with other jurisdictions	3.4	21	3.5	15	3.6	16	3.4	19
	Multilateral audits in collaboration with other jurisdictions	3.1	25	2.7	25	3.2	25	3.0	25

Note: Results for the question, 'Which of the following tools has enhanced or could enhance certainty in the tax system?' The respondents could choose from a scale from 5 to 1, where 5 is the specific tool has increased or could increase certainty substantially, and lower numbers where the tool is progressively less important. Not all respondents scored each factor, the number of responses per factor is recorded in the Obs column. The Rank column indicates the ranking (1-21) of each factor for each region

Source: OECD (2016) Tax certainty survey

Annex C. Methodology

The results and analysis used in this report draws upon three different exercises.

Survey of tax administration official perceptions of MNEs/large business and Big Four tax behaviour

The results obtained for the publication were based on a perception survey carried out by the OECD in English, French, Spanish and Arabic during the last quarter of 2019 and first quarter of 2020. The survey was disseminated among tax officials participating in OECD's Global Relations events and trainings, as well as by requesting OECD country representatives to distribute it among officials from their Administrations. Although the survey was anonymous, respondents were asked to identify their country, function / unit, years of experience, and field.

The survey aimed to capture the perceptions that tax officials have on the tax behaviour of large/multinational companies, and on the Big Four consulting firms. The 'Big Four' are the four largest consulting and auditing companies (Deloitte, KPMG, EY and PricewaterhouseCoopers).

The survey was based on responsible tax principles and voluntary codes of conduct adopted by businesses, more specifically, on the Business at OECD Statement of Tax Best Practices for Engaging with Tax Authorities in Developing Countries (Business at OECD, 2013[1]) and on the Codes of Conduct for Responsible Tax Practice, where available, from the Big Four (not all the Big Four have such codes of conduct). These principles and codes of conduct outline the standards of behaviour expected in a range of areas including compliance, communication, and transparency.

The survey was then divided into two sections, the first one concerning perceptions of MNEs/large business behaviour and the second one referring to the behaviour of Big Four firms. For the MNEs/large business, the survey addressed the following issues:

- **Transparency and trust**
- **Dispute resolution**
- **Political lobbying**
- **Staff retention**
- **Responsiveness to requests**
- **Timeliness of payments**
- **Bribery**
- **Views on voluntary principles**
- **Commitment to cooperation**
- **Tax incentives**
- **Public commitment to taxation**
- **Behaviour compared to local business**

Regarding the Big Four firms, the survey mainly focused on the following issues.

- **Transparency and trust**
- **Role in recruitment**
- **Staff retention**

- **Aggressiveness/spirit of the law**
- **Influence on client behaviour**
- **Behaviour vis-à-vis local advisors**

For further details, please see the complete survey in the following link: https://www.oecd.org/tax/tax-global/survey-business-big-four-tax-practices-engagement.pdf

The survey was answered by 1 240 officials (most of them tax auditors) working in Tax Administrations in 138 countries. The results have been grouped by regional averages; Africa (34 countries, 206 responses), Asia (31 countries, 372 responses), LAC (30 countries, 325 responses) and OECD regions (25 countries, 225 responses). The regional groups are in line with the approach taken in previous work in the OECD tax morale and tax certainty literature (see (OECD, 2019[2])). The data have been smoothed to ensure that no country is over-represented in the sample, with a maximum weighting of one country of 10% per region.

Several sensitivity exercises were undertaken to ensure the robustness of the results. For instance, age and rank were controlled for as to see if the results varied with age or position. Once these variable were controlled for, the results continued to hold.

Tax certainty survey

Previous results from the tax certainty work (see (IMF/OECD, 2017[3]), (IMF/OECD, 2018[4]) and (OECD, 2019[2]), and its corresponding survey and results were also used to complement the perceptions of tax administrators. The aim of the tax certainty survey was to explore the nature of tax uncertainty, its main sources and effects on business decisions, and obtain a set of concrete and practical approaches to help policymakers and tax administrations shape a more certain tax environment.

The survey was circulated using the OECD network of government officials, tax practitioners, civil society and businesses, including the OECD's Business Industry Advisory Committee (BIAC). The survey was open between October and December 2016 and received 724 responses from firms headquartered in 62 different countries. Country-specific responses were also aggregated by region (Africa, Asia, LAC and OECD). This approach provides significantly different numbers of observations in each region, and also has significantly different numbers of observations per country, though in no region was the most frequent country chosen by respondents responsible for more than 35% of responses.

Roundtables

To complement the empirical results provided by both surveys, a set of virtual regional roundtables were organized between December 2020 and May 2021:

- LAC Roundtable on Tax Morale (18-20 May 2021)
- African Roundtable on Tax Morale (27-28 April 2021)
- OECD/IOTA Roundtable on Tax Morale (20 January 2021)
- Asia Roundtable on Tax Morale (7-8 December 2020)

The meetings were co-hosted by the OECD and key regional partners including the IOTA, CIAT, ATAF, the Study Group on Asian Tax Administration and Research (SGATAR) and the Asian Development Bank (ADB).

The roundtables gathered Administrations, MNEs operating in the region, tax professionals and relevant business associations. Its goal was to facilitate a dialogue between businesses and governments to discuss in more depth the findings of the surveys, focusing on identifying key issues for both MNEs and Tax Authorities, and potential tools and approaches to use going forward, all participants received a background document with a summary of results, and an initial analysis of the key findings relevant to the region, this was complemented by a presentation provided by the OECD secretariat on the survey results. The rest of the roundtables consisted of a combination of moderated panel discussions and breakout room discussions. Over 150 participants from Africa, 160 from IOTA member countries, 160 from LAC, and 130 participants from Asia attended these roundtables. With delegates from nearly 100 countries in total participating.

References

Business at OECD (2013), *BIAC Statement of Tax Best Practices for Engaging with Tax Authorities in Developing Countries*, https://biac.org/wp-content/uploads/2020/11/Statement-of-Tax-Best-Practices-for-Engaging-with-Tax-Authorities-in-Developing-Countries-Original-release-Sep-2013-1.pdf. [1]

IMF/OECD (2018), *Update on Tax Certainty: IMF/OECD Report for the G20 Finance Ministers and Central Bank Governors*, https://www.oecd.org/tax/tax-policy/tax-certainty-update-oecd-imf-report-g20-finance-ministers-july-2018.pdf. [4]

IMF/OECD (2017), *Tax Certainty: IMF/OECD Report for the G20 Finance Ministers*, https://www.oecd.org/tax/tax-policy/tax-certainty-report-oecd-imf-report-g20-finance-ministers-march-2017.pdf. [3]

OECD (2019), *Tax Morale: What Drives People and Businesses to Pay Tax?*, OECD Publishing, Paris, https://doi.org/10.1787/f3d8ea10-en. [2]

www.ingramcontent.com/pod-product-compliance
Lightning Source LLC
Chambersburg PA
CBHW082111210326
41599CB00033B/6665